Recollections and Reflections

by

Lois Baldwin DeVoe

Copyright © 2020 by Lois Baldwin DeVoe

All rights reserved. No part of this book may be reprinted or reproduced without the permission of the author.

ISBN 978-1-62806-311-0   (print | paperback)

Library of Congress Control Number 2021904994

Published by Salt Water Media
29 Broad Street, Suite 104
Berlin, MD 21811
www.saltwatermedia.com

Cover design by Richard Deurer
Interior images provided by the author

• *Dedication* •

This book is dedicated to my nephew and Godson, Andrew Kahl, who started me on the project, and to my children, Nancy and Streett, without whose encouragement I never would have finished it.

Note from the Author

In my youthful life, there were certain rules about behavior, clothing, make-up and dating. These rules were enforced, up to a point, by our mothers, and we dared not disobey them. I give you some of the most important ones here, so that you may better understand the cultural climate in which I grew up.

No white shoes or pants after Labor Day. Indeed, we didn't even call them pants, but slacks. if they were the dressy kind. We wore blue jeans on occasion, but they were never permitted in the dining rooms of young ladies' colleges. We got around that one by keeping a skirt in the coatroom, which was then pulled on over the rolled-up jeans. One wore a hat to church, and white gloves for downtown shopping even in the heat of summer. Heels were never to be worn with pants, for risk of being considered a tramp. Cleavage was a definite no-no, and a strapless dress, while okay for the prom, required a strapless bra just to assure its modesty and discomfort.

In elementary school, my mother made me wear long, thick stockings (and a skirt, of course) to keep my legs warm. My rebellion on this issue came about very early. I arrived at the saddle shoe and penny loafer stage at about seventh grade, which then necessitated bobby socks and knee-length skirts. This was our uniform through high school, except for dress-up occasions when we got out the garter belts and nylons, or even the actual girdles, the most uncomfortable undergarment ever invented.

Make-up consisted of lipstick. Period. Maybe a little powder. But any girl wearing eyeliner or blush risked ostracism and would doubtless be labeled loose. Hair was worn parted on the side and anchored by a silver barrette. And keep your natural color! When I reached my thirties, my friends and I would apply a tiny upstroke of dark eyebrow pencil to the outer corners of our eyes. Very daring.

Ah, the dating rules. No open-mouth kissing; no touching allowed below the neck or above the knees, and you definitely did not touch boys below the navel. There were so many ways to get pregnant that we scared ourselves to death and made a fetish out of preserving our virginity -- but we broke a lot of the rules along the way. I learned the f-word at about thirteen, when one of my classmates was sent to a girls' reform school for "doing it." Apparently she got caught in the act, but I never learned what happened to the boy involved. Probably nothing, considering the times.

It was simply not done for a girl to call a boy on the phone. You waited until he made the first move, always. But I remember juggling dates and my mother being complicit in my deceitfulness as I would break one date in favor of a more desirable one. Although she clucked and tsk-tsk'ed about it, she was really amused at the machinations and we laughed about it in later years.

Don't get me started on the table manners. Oh well, yes, do get me started. What has happened to table manners? And table settings? We even had instructions in school about where to place the knife, the fork, the extra forks, the spoons, the napkin (linen or damask, naturally), the bread and butter plate, the salad plate, the water goblet and anything else that had a rightful position on a dining table. We waited for everyone else to be served, and until the hostess lifted her fork, before we could dig in, and we never left the table until excused, whining and fidgeting notwithstanding. Elbows off the table! Sit up straight! Never push the peas onto the fork with your knife, and always move fork to right hand after cutting a bite with fork in left hand. How liberating to observe, in Europe, food entering mouths from a fork held in the left hand after slicing the bite!

Males were never allowed to wear baseball caps at dinner. Or any other kind of cap or hat in the house. Too bad about your hat hair.

Finally, and this current custom really irks: the proper response to "thank you" is "you're welcome" not "no problem." Which brings up one I had almost forgotten: a gift required an actual hand-written thank-you note. I am immensely please when our great-grandchildren follow this one, evidence that all is not lost in the realm of good manners.

So this was life in early-to-mid twentieth century America. In a way, I'm sorry it has changed so much.

Chapter 1

When I reached the over-ripe age of eighty-three or so, I realized that I might possibly never write the Great American Novel. I had been side-tracked by life itself, darting here and there like a butterfly, or a moth, always avoiding the hard work of actually writing the novel. It took nudging from some loved ones who wanted to string together some family threads, to provide the motivation. Maybe this will prod them into doing the same for their own loved ones, so that the fabric itself can be preserved.

It has been a good life, not without its bumps, but a happy one. I haven't accomplished a fraction of what I dreamed of doing. I've been a lifeguard, a sales clerk, an insurance company typist, receptionist and switchboard operator, a fashion model, a teacher, a real estate agent, a staffer with the House Un-American Activities Committee in the U.S. Congress, (for a Democrat like me at the time, that was quite the experience), a secretary both legal and judicial, an arts administrator, wardrobe consultant, wife, mother, and volunteer in problems of the aging. I've enjoyed amateur acting and singing. I sampled a little politics as an officer in the Young Democrats of Baltimore County and Maryland, and almost ran for public office. I've made serious mistakes and detours along the way but, looking back, I can see where the challenges and veerings, the opportunities and disappointments lay, and how they converged to push me in the directions I took. I would change some things if I could; others would remain as they are, especially the people in my life who are so dear to me. I can only mourn the lost ones who helped to shape that life.

My parents were both born and raised in Baltimore. Mother, Marion Sayford Meese, was a student at Western High School and Dad, Christian Henry Kahl, was attending the Polytechnic Institute of Baltimore when they met, through her brother Norman. The two boys had become acquainted through athletic connection between Poly and City, which Norman was attending. I've been told that Dad pursued my mother ardently from the beginning, but she though him too young at two year her junior, and resisted his advances for several years. She graduated from high school and went to work as a secretary at a dental lab, still living at home with her parents on Marx Avenue in the northeastern section of the city. In those days, the location was suburban, with lawns and trees and park-like areas nearby.

Dad was not to be put off. He had left school before graduating, in order to help support his family. My paternal grandfather, Christian Frederick Marion George Kahl, established himself early as a good-time fellow with an insatiable craving for alcoholic beverages, and was never able to hold a job for very long — despite the needs of a wife and six children. My grandmother, Agnes Price Kahl, was from a Scots-Irish background who married my grandfather while still in her teens, and never worked outside the home. My dad had a paper route as a young boy, and later became a copywriter for the Baltimore Sun. A natural talent for writing was the basis for his early dream of writing for Hollywood. He was also good with numbers, learned accounting on his own and by enrolling in a correspondence course based at the Wharton School in Philadelphia. He later parlayed that skill into management positions.

Meanwhile, however, Mother was still resisting because of his youth. There was also the issue of socio-economic level. Family lore has it that one of the maternal great-grandfathers was wealthy enough to have staked the original Hires Root Beer creator to his first manufacturing of the beverage, but thought it would never succeed and sold his share for five hundred dollars. This doesn't show up in Ancestry.com, but what the website does reveal is that my maternal great-grandfather, Jacob Wells Meese, served in the 45th Regiment Pennsylvania Infantry during the Civil War, rising to the rank of 1st. Lieutenant. Research by other family members has also turned up a connection to Samuel Adams, who had married Rebecca Wells, and the Wells name was carried on not only through Jacob Wells Meese, but into succeeding generations. So it seems there may have been a hint of snobbery here.

Dad worked hard to build himself a socially acceptable persona, cultivating friendships with successful businessmen who took him under their wings and taught him about hobbies such as yachting, golf, tennis and horseback riding. His childhood, while mostly poor in material things, had nevertheless been enriched by his mother's insistence on good manners, clean clothes and an ironed handkerchief in his pocket every day, as well as training in fair play and consideration for others.

His father possessed musical talent and intelligence; both attributes were significant when he was sober enough to contribute as a parent. There were also several aunts, sisters of Christian Frederick Marion George, who doted on their brother and his brood, and who had "married well", producing companionable, refined cousins for the Kahls. Two of those cousins, John and Francis Linn, entered the Catholic priesthood, one later becoming the President of St. Charles College in Catonsville, Maryland (an institution later to become the Charlestown Retirement Community). Of the Biemiller brothers, one became a dentist, and the other a chiropractor. The dentist was the one who installed the braces on my teeth, which remain stubbornly crooked to this day. In present times, of course, a specialist would have been employed for the task. Only today I have been examined by an endodontist to whom I was sent by my dentist, and she is sending me to a periodontist for further evaluation. In my childhood, one guy did it all. Also, I can never recall hearing of a female dentist!

Eventually, as Chris's fortunes improved, my mother and her family decided to accept him, and the two became engaged. They married on July 3rd, 1926, one day after Dad turned 21, and moved into the Meese home on Marx Avenue, which is the site of my earliest childhood memories. Mother was to celebrate her 23rd birthday on July 29th. They became members of the Maryland Yacht Club with their sailing canoe, a popular boat in those days, and I'm told that I was conceived in that canoe. Hard to imagine, considering the inherent instability of such watercraft.

When I was three, during the Great Depression which was beginning to stretch over the nation, my dad was lucky enough to find a job as bookkeeper to a company called Belber Trunk and Bag. How the memory of this has stuck with me I do not know, but I remember living in Woodbury, New Jersey and walking with my mother to the nearby Piggly-Wiggly grocery. I also recall being terrorized by neighborhood kids taking me through a cemetery. Happily, we stayed there for only a year or two before returning to Baltimore where Dad had found new employment. He was among the lucky ones, never being without a job during that entire era, and we had my grandparents' Marx Avenue house to return to after our stay in New Jersey.

The Meese home, by that time, had become a scene of turmoil as my grandmother, nee Clara Arnold, suffered her first bout with mental illness - never properly diagnosed but determined in hindsight to have been manic-depressive psychosis. There were no drugs available for treatment at the time, while today this condition, now known as bi-polar disorder, is easily controlled by modern medicine. Her husband, my grandfather Edgar Wells Meese, a freighter captain, would be gone at sea for six or seven months at a time. In her manic state, my grandmother did a lot of shopping - including cars. One was a Hupmobile (which I faintly remember), jewelry and other luxury items, with the money he sent home. My grandmother was eventually hospitalized at the mental institution Springfield in Sykesville, Maryland, where she later died of pneumonia. My recollections of her are rather dim and few. I do remember her as seeming aloof and not affectionate, unlike my other grandmother, Agnes, with her ready smile and sweet disposition.

How that lady managed to keep her sanity and her sweet disposition has always amazed me. One frightening memory of my paternal grandfather storming into the house, cursing and slamming doors, remains with me today. But Grandma would tolerate no criticism of her "Chrissie" and she managed her six youngsters with a velvet glove. She could never understand my complaints about my own two when they got on my nerves. When Chrissie had a stroke and went into the nursing home, she visited him constantly and loved the man until he died. I believe a strong faith in her church must have been her salvation. This was most certainly true when her second son, Louis, committed suicide together with his girlfriend by turning on a gas stove in an apartment where they were found. I never knew the circumstances that drove them to this desperate act.

Chapter 2

How did "Pop" become a seafaring man? Well, it seems that when he was a boy in Harrisburg, Pennsylvania, he and his two brothers, the older Horace and the younger Norman, lived a happy, carefree life, swimming in the Susquehanna River and getting an education in the public schools of the city. Edgar, however, turned out to be a less than enthusiastic student as time went on, and his father, Jacob Wells Meese, advised all three of them that if they did not apply themselves enough to go to college, they would be sent to join the Merchant Marine on a school ship. That, to his father's surprise and chagrin, was exactly what Edgar wanted, and so off he went to begin his career on a sailing schooner as a lowly apprentice. Recently I went through some of the papers he had left behind, which I had kept in a small train case along with papers and other souvenirs from my mother, and found something that seemed to indicate that he had spent three years in the U.S. Navy. Could the Merchant Marine have been a part, then, of the Navy? Perhaps in my occasional spurts of family research at Ancestry.com, I may solve this mystery.

I often asked him about those days, whether he had eaten "hardtack" and he said that he had, but I have no idea to this day what exactly it is. I know that he learned to sail the hard way on a big schooner similar to what we call today a "tall ship", and that he gradually worked his way up until he earned his master's license. As Captain, he worked for at least two shipping companies out of New York, one being the American-West African Line. My memory recalls a ship named the *S.S. West Kebar*, and one other called the *S.S. Otho*.

When I was a teenager, I begged him to take me with him on a voyage to the exotic foreign ports he talked about - the Canary Islands, Italy, the African continent, especially the Congo River, although I don't know why his ship took a voyage up the famous African river. It being a freighter, the cargo could have been ivory, ebony wood, native African products, furs, but surely not slaves. That trade was long over by the time he took control of a ship. He always arrived home with gifts: native art objects, rugs made of animal pelts, teakwood lamps, brass trays, even French perfume.

Once, two of the dozen or so passengers allowed onboard were Martin and Osa Johnson, a married pair of explorers who at the time were quite well-known. And Pop enjoyed their company very much. On another trip, he brought home the first of a pair of chimpanzees - a male named Charlie who was only permitted a short stay by my mother at our home. Charlie then was donated to the Baltimore Zoo, where Charlie exhibited much resentment. We frequently visited him at the zoo, and on one occasion Charlie reached through the bars of his cage and seized Pop's pocket watch, which he then swung around his head and flung at the bars. The watch survived the ordeal, as I recall my grandfather consulting it many times afterward. Another visit ended in disaster as Charlie vomited through the cage bars all over Pop's white summer suit. I guess one could say he was not happy in captivity. Or perhaps he missed Pop's companionship. On the next trip, Pop brought a mate for Charlie, which proved to be an inspired solution. He and his new companion, Susie, found happiness together, living long and healthy lives in the care of the zoo.

Two other Pop stories are vivid in my memory: on one trip he had a cook who went berserk and started chasing another crew member with a butcher knife, and had to be subdued. I don't know whether it was Pop or someone else who did the subduing, but it must have been a scary scene to be at sea under the circumstances. The other has to do with furs. When I was about twelve, he brought my mother a batch of brown, thick, warm pelts from a small African antelope called the hyrax. In the center of each fur was a light golden streak. There were enough skins to make a coat for my mother, and she had her furrier save the rest to later make a coat for me which I took to college and later for two years to Europe. It only gave out after I had divorced and remarried and was living in Towson, with my second husband and our two small children. Tough furs! The leopard skins which he brought on another occasion had not been properly tanned in Africa, and they had to be destroyed while we were still on the farm in Reisterstown. I think Mother and I would both have been embarrassed to wear leopard skins, given the beginnings of concern for the welfare of these beautiful animals. But back to the hyrax - many years later I made the acquaintance of a big-game hunter who claimed there was no such creature, so it gave me enormous pleasure to prove him wrong by checking it out in the World Book Encyclopedia To add to my pleasure, my daughter returned recently from a trip to Africa, where she actually saw hyraxes and was able to capture a photo of them while on a game drive.

Chapter 3

During the first World War, my grandfather was persuaded to take a leave of absence after his ship ran into some kind of dangerous situation at sea involving a German submarine or warship, I'm not sure which. He took a job with the Customs House in Baltimore for the duration of the war, but was back at the work he loved soon after the Armistice. His career lasted until about 1934, when he and my parents decided to buy a farm together. I found out much later that he had spent many long days and nights at sea reading about farming and learning how to be a farmer. This knowledge was extremely valuable when the thirty-six acres of land they purchased in Reisterstown became a working farm, with two mules, a cow, a vegetable garden, some chickens and pigs, a sizeable apple orchard and a neglected asparagus patch which he brought back to life. Cornfields blossomed, the old apple orchard began to yield again, and there was even a grape arbor from which we could possibly have made some wine if anybody had known anything about wine-making. They named the place Marlo Farm, using my name and my mother's, although my uncle, the comedian, wanted to call it Seven Elderberry Bushes.

Two years after we moved from the city, when I was seven, my most special Christmas present that year was a little brother. Chris was born on December 21, 1935 in Baltimore City, and I was allowed to hold him all the way home from the hospital, wearing my brand-new tan coat and matching hat. It was like holding a living doll, and I couldn't wait to start treating him like one at home. After he became a toddler, it was great fun for me, if not for him, to dress him up in various costumes and makeshift wigs, a mop perhaps. There are pictures somewhere of the disgruntled little boy so attired.

While Chris was still an infant, my mother's brother, Norman, brought his baby girl and himself to live with us after the tragic death of his young wife, Anne. Her little daughter, Betty Anne, was only three months old when her mother passed away, at the age of twenty-nine, from a mysterious illness for which she had been hospitalized and, we learned many years later, misdiagnosed. I had admired my beautiful Aunt Anne so much that I treasured her photograph for many years before finally giving it to her daughter, who by then was married and a mother herself. Later, I chose the diminutive of her name, Nancy, to bestow upon my own daughter. But back then my mother had two babies to care for, with little assistance from me at that age. Fortunately, we had a housekeeper who lived with us, as well as a young girl from the neighborhood who came several days each week to help with the housework.

We also had a "hired man" to help with the farm work, who resided in a one-room log cabin near the smokehouse. I have never figured out what he did for a bathroom, as there wasn't one in the cabin, just a wood stove, a bed, chair and bureau on the first floor, and nothing in the attic above. I was always trying to start a flower garden around the little house, to cheer things up a bit, but was never very successful.

Every now and then we'd have a visit from one or the other of Pop's brothers - my great-uncles, Horace or Norman. Horace and his wife, Frances (Aunt Frank) lived in New York City, where he was involved in the world of finance. I have no idea what he did for a living, but he wore spats, (very strange-looking cuffs over his shoes), and carried a walking stick which, I'm sure, was an affection. Aunt Frank once brought me a silk blouse designed for an adult woman. I was eight or nine at the time, but I treasured that gift until I was old enough to wear it.

Great-uncle Norman would come with his wife, Aunt Genevieve, and their two sons, who were close enough to my age to be interesting to me. Norman was always full of mischief; Kenny and I tagged along and got into trouble with him, but that never stopped us. I adored my cousins, spending many happy vacations at their home in Kensington, a suburb of the nation's capital. There were swimming, boys, dancing, tennis, and street games in the evenings, and it was from that home that I saw both cousins off to serve in World War II. Kenny stepped on a land mine in Europe, sustaining injuries that plagued him all his life, while Norman came home afterward unscathed. On an interesting side note, Aunt Genevieve had served in the WAC, Women's Army Corps, during World War I, and is buried at Arlington National Cemetery.

I think that Pop went back to sea for a while during this period, because our day girl's father came to do the milking. When war broke out in 1941, my mother was able to persuade him to retire again. Crossing the Atlantic had by then become truly hazardous, and he finally gave it up to come home permanently.

Eventually, both the housekeeper and the hired hand left us to go to work in defense factories, and working the farm became very difficult. Mother was complaining daily about having to wash the multiple tiny parts of the cream separator, by hand, for of course dishwashers were still unheard-of at the time. When I was just shy of thirteen, my mother had her first bout with the same illness that had haunted her mother for most of her life. Mother was hospitalized for a "nervous breakdown" and it fell to me to haltingly take charge of things at home, with the assistance of a neighbor's somewhat older daughter. Together, the rest of us survived the ordeal. Little did I know that the event and its sequels would play such a large part in defining my own life. At the time, I also had no knowledge of the family history of this horrific disease, which had also affected my grandmother's Uncle Alfred. Tracing the threads of it as I grew older became a fascinating, frightening pursuit which hounds me still today. In many ways, I blundered through life searching for ways to avoid the insanity which had befallen so much of my family.

For my part, however, there are many wonderful memories of growing up on the farm. We had a couple of horses, retired from the racetrack, and I was allowed to use the curry comb on their glistening hides. Mucking out stalls was not so bad, when one was then allowed to take a ride. I joined the 4-H Club and, for a project, raised a little Berkshire pig I named Isabel, who when grown produced a beautiful litter of piglets. I watched their births first-hand, while Pop swabbed each little navel with iodine as they came into the world. There were quite a few, although I don't remember how many. I do know that we exhibited Isabel at the State Fair, where she won a blue ribbon and was then purchased by a woman from our area, Mrs. Charles Williams. Years later, I happened to meet her somewhere and inquired about my sow. I was immensely relieved to hear that she had died of honorable old age, having produced many fine litters for her new owner. I also had rabbits, kept in a cage in a shed near the barn, and a wonderful dog named Butch, who was a St. Bernard mixed with German Shepherd. He went everywhere with me, loping along beside my bike and protecting me from any dangers – be they other dogs or suspicious-looking people. When I went to the movie theatre he would stand guard by my bike until I came out. He was beloved by all of our barn cats, too, who curled up around and on top of him at night, keeping warm. Butch also played sentinel, making the rounds of all the farm buildings while we slept. On hot summer nights, Chris and I slept on a second-floor screened porch, from which we could hear the dog checking things out below.

Our chickens were White Leghorns. The hens laid and guarded their eggs, while my job was to reach under their fluffy white bellies and take the eggs from them. This was often resented, so that I was frequently pecked at, and clucked at, so it was not a chore that I especially enjoyed. The grownups had had a new chicken house built when we moved to the place and, before the chickens moved in, they threw a mint julep party in the new building. Dad was at that time general manager of the Greenspring Valley Hunt Club, (both clubs - the horsey one and the golfing one), and I remember dozens of frosted glasses filled with ice being kept chilled in a large refrigerator brought in for the purpose. I also remember one very sad night when the brooder house caught fire and several hundred baby chicks died; fire engines came screaming down our lane, the whole night lit up with the flames from the little structure, and in the air was the smell of charred little chick bodies. It broke my heart.

Later, as is often the case in farm life, rats found their way into various places, the corn crib and the chicken house among them. Pop would let me go with him as he attacked the ones in the chicken house with his 16-gauge shotgun. We'd sit silently waiting, at the door of the chickens' habitat, until a rat poked his head up from a hole by one of the poles inside, then POW! he'd be gone. After shooting as many as he could, my grandfather then filled up the hole with cement and the chickens could live in peace for a while.

Other jobs for me included thinning the corn when it was very young and just sprouting from neat rows in the field. This had to be done by hand, and it was meant to insure that the remaining plants would grow up strong and hearty, and give a better yield. When we were in asparagus season, I'd take a long, special two-pronged knife, cutting the asparagus stalks just below the surface of the soil, making sure to cut only the most tender ones. Then I'd put them into a little hand tool, a rounded container with circling arms to enclose the proper number of spears. This gadget had a cutter at one end that would slice off the tough ends of the spears, making them all even, and then we tied the bundles in two places with a special flat string that wouldn't pierce the delicate green flesh of the fresh vegetable – which was then ready to go to market.

On Sundays, we'd have chicken for dinner and homemade ice cream. Whoever did the churning got to lick the paddles. We also churned our own butter during the war, avoiding the yellow-dyed margarine required by rationing rules.

I didn't spend a lot of time in the house in those days. Arriving home from school, I'd take a book and climb the tree over Isabel's pen where I could watch her eating, drinking from her water trough and rolling around in the mud. Or, I would be following Pop around, learning how to be a farmer. The 4-H Club was very active then, and I enjoyed being a member, raising my pig and sewing clothes from feed sacks. Isabel got her blue ribbon just for being who she was, and one year I got a blue ribbon for a two-piece dress I'd made from feed sacks which I had dyed a deep sienna color. The Girl Scouts were another of my pursuits, and I belonged to a troop in Reisterstown along with several friends. I was not the most enthusiastic badge earner, much preferring the tap-dancing classes that were offered as a substitute for ballet in our small rural community. I was never very good at that either, and soon gave it up for more exciting activities. I discovered singing and found that I could carry a tune. Our maternal great-grandmother had been a piano teacher; Uncle Norman played the saxophone well enough to be in a local band, and our mother was an accomplished pianist and also played the organ. Cousin Betty Anne, too, played piano and organ, so I guess you could say it was in the genes. I joined the Peabody Junior Choir, and we sang a Christmas concert at the Walters Art Gallery, wearing green satin robes with large cream collars, and carrying candles. I also sang in our Episcopalian church's junior choir, where my mother served as substitute organist and Dad as Lay Reader.

At the tender age of about ten, I was taken by my parents to my first opera – The Barber of Seville – which sowed the seeds for a lifetime of loving classical music. This was also helped by my father's enthusiasm for that musical genre. Many summer evenings at home were filled with the sounds of Debussy, Ravel, Rachmaninoff, Beethoven, Tchaikowsky, Wagner, and others of the great masters as Dad played their recordings for us. Later, Chris and I used to love pretending that we were conductors during these performances, wielding imaginary batons as we coaxed the lovely melodies from our imaginary musicians.

Piano lessons were also a big part of my life at the time. My teacher, Mr. Susemihl, was the grandfather of one of my best friends, Susie. He came to the house for my lessons, like our doctor, who never hesitated to make house calls. I was not very good at practicing, and consequently never became very good at playing the instrument.

Susie reminded me, a few years ago, of some pleasant childhood memories when she visited me at the farm. We were commissioned by Pop to catch corn beetles in a jar and bring them to him. He paid us a penny for each beetle we captured. Susie also remembers my mother allowing the two of us to play with her bottles and jars of beauty products. She said, "You and I and your beautiful mom, playing with all the make-up she had sent away for, for us".

My own "sending away for" extended to chameleons, which promptly passed away in my care, but I kept trying because I was fascinated by their ability to change color depending upon where you placed them. I also loved Nancy Drew mysteries and tried many of her tricks to track down evil-doers. A select group of us could often be found searching an old abandoned house for clues, using the fingerprint dust I had also sent away for. We never caught any criminals nor, in fact, did we uncover any crimes, but it was good practice for the sleuthing future we imagined for ourselves.

Some of my friends and I formed a bicycle club soon after I got my first bike as a gift for my eighth birthday. It was Dad's suggestion, after he'd taught me to ride. The group consisted of four or five close friends, Bobbie Schmall, Sarah Jean Fuss, Betty Jean Tovell, Ann Caltrider, Patsy Reese, and occasionally a couple of others. We cycled freely around the neighborhood and beyond, without helmets and completely out of communication with our mothers – until we were expected home in time for dinner. We also spent time, once, in a swimming hole on one neighbor's farm, where I had my first, and only, encounter with leeches. We were fearless when it came to snakes and other wildlife, and barking dogs, but not with leeches. It was after that episode that I pleaded for, and won, a season pass to the Glyndon Swim Club, where I spent many happy summers growing up.

When it came time for high school, I resisted my parents' attempts to push me into a private school, Hannah More, claiming that I would be heartbroken to leave my friends at Franklin High. Although I won that battle after much pleading and whining, brother Chris lost his skirmish and was enrolled at McDonogh, then a military academy for boys, complete with uniforms and horses. He attained the rank of lieutenant before finally winning his little war and being allowed to return to Franklin. In some ways, I think we would both have been better prepared for college had we heeded our parents' wishes; I could also have had my fill of horse-life at Hannah More. But we all know that hindsight is 20/20.

At fifteen, I was hired by my dad to fill the job of lifeguard at the Greenspring Club. This turn of fortune was made possible by the shortage of boys at the time. So many of them had gone to war that no one questioned the presence of a girl at the post. I was minimally qualified, having taken a basic life-saving course and being a fairly decent swimmer. That was a lovely, carefree summer, spent lounging around the pool and trying to make the kids behave. My salary was free swimming and free lunch delivered poolside by a white-coated black waiter.

My high school boyfriend was one of those who left school to join the armed services. In his case, it was the Army Air Corps. He had an exotic family, owners of a traveling circus, who spent their winters in a rented home in Pikesville. Charles and his brother, Julian, were both trapeze artists and musicians. Charles played the trumpet. Although he left before graduation, his photo appears in our yearbook, in uniform. Nearly every evening while in basic training, he would call me from Madison, Wisconsin. I remember that we fought constantly while he was still in school, but those phone conversations were a different matter. Time, separation, meeting other boys and going off to college gradually ended the relationship.

During World War II Dad offered his services as an air raid warden, which meant checking the neighborhood to be sure everyone was blacked out – shades drawn, no car lights or other illumination whenever there was a drill. He and I rode our bikes on these occasions, and I felt very important helping with the war effort. We also saved aluminum foil and endured rationing of meat, gas and other supplies. We had always churned our own butter, although there was an occasional attempt to use margarine, which required adding yellow color to the inedible stuff that was available. Victory gardens were popular, as people raised their own vegetables and became more self-sufficient in doing so. Sometimes we students offered ourselves as pickers of fruits or vegetables for other local farmers whose help had gone off either to fight or work in defense plants. I have one very uncomfortable memory of severe sunburn after picking strawberries all day – without sunscreen, of course; who knew what we now know about sun damage? – and going to a formal school dance that evening in excruciating pain. Not to mention the puffed red face that no amount of powder could conceal.

Chapter 4

By this time, well into the war, Marlo Farm had become too much for Pop. Dad was ever the gentleman farmer who never had mastered the art of milking a cow, although he had cleverly converted an old car into a pick-up truck for collecting the apples in our orchard and had also invented a pole-mounted basket for reaching the highest ones. He had, in fact, entered the world of politics from which he never really returned, becoming first Clerk of the Court for Baltimore County, then member and Chair of the three-man Board of County Commissioners. Late, after voter acceptance of the so-called charter form of county government, he became the first elected County Executive of Baltimore County. Consequently, I knew all about potholes, water in basements, sewage treatment plants and getting voters to the polls at a very early age. Thanks to the acquisition of a real estate broker's license, as well as one for insurance sales, our dad made a good living outside of the political arena, but he had always dreamed of public life; he just knew it was not a path to financial success - at least in those times. However, it being after World War II with abundant opportunities for growth and change, he succeeded in creating many reforms and updates in county government.

My uncle had full-time employment and was not inclined toward the farming life anyway, and had re-married about this time, moving out and taking his little girl with him. It appeared to be a practical solution to sell the farm and move to a house much closer to our town, a move which pleased me enormously as I had now become a teen-ager in high school, with all of the needs and desires of the species. Pop had taught me first to drive the tractor, (which had replaced the mules, Sis and Toddy), and later his truck, so I was ready as soon as I turned sixteen to hit the road as a licensed driver.

With access to my mother's wooden-sided Ford station wagon, I became the chauffeur for my high school gang; with a portable radio and some beer lifted from someone's unsuspecting parents, we spent quite a few evenings parked and partying in a local field we called Dogpatch. Another tidbit from Susie recalls the two of us driving around at night, with me at the wheel, going through a secluded lovers' lane, and shouting out of the window, "God sees you!" Interesting that my husband, Bob, remembers doing the exact same thing as a teenager in Cleveland, Ohio.

The years in that new house were good ones except for my mother's regular lapses into mental illness. I started dating from there; I left for college from there. Pop gave me my first cigarette in that house, an unfiltered Camel, insisting that I finish it, so of course I got sick and had no more desire for a smoke until several years later. He also warned me about "reefers", not to take cigarettes from strangers because they might contain some toxic substance like marijuana - which nobody had ever heard of then. I remember a post-and-rail fence around the back of the lot, and our neighbor, Brooke Pierce, throwing stones at my window to get me out to ride with him. I was a horse nut in those days, and for years afterward, always taking horseback riding for Physical Education in college and always hoping one day to have my own farm where I could have my own horse and ride every day.

It was while we were living in that house that Jack Biemiller, Dad's dentist cousin, called one day to say that he had a nice saddle horse he needed to get rid of, and asked if I would like to have it. No longer did we have a barn, with stalls and hay and all those other horse requirements, but I would ask around the neighborhood as soon as I got home from school; which I did, and successfully, as the farmer across Berryman's Lane from us agreed that I could rent a stall from him and keep my horse there. Dad gave his consent, as I think he kind of wanted to get on a horse once in a while too, and I'm guessing he'd agreed to help me pay for this venture, because I had nothing but babysitting funds for income. However, by the time I'd made all the arrangements, Cousin Jack had called back and informed my mother that he had another willing recipient and had already let the animal go. I was, to say the least, devastated and have never forgotten this disappointment. One of my most frequent dreams for years after was of coming home from school, going to the stable for my horse, and galloping across open fields for hours.

Also during those years, the Nancy Lee came into our lives: a 36-foot wooden cabin cruiser that we berthed at the Sparrows Point Yacht Club. The boat had a galley and a head, both very primitive by today's standards, and she could accommodate the four of us plus, later, my college boyfriend. A devout Catholic, John was obligated to attend Mass on Sundays, so we always found ourselves anchored out on Saturday nights in the vicinity of a Catholic church so that John and I could row ashore in the dinghy and fulfill that obligation. For bathing from the boat, we jumped overboard with a bar of Ivory soap (it floated) into what was then an unpolluted Chesapeake Bay. Obviously, we knew nothing about pollution at the time, as we were among the offenders. Dad's favorite saying, as we took off from the dock, was "Batten down the beer."

When the family vacations took place in Ocean City, as they frequently did, my life was pure joy. We stayed in an apartment building at the corner of Ninth Street and Baltimore Avenue, which contained a ground-floor room immediately claimed by me. The rest of the family stayed on the first floor just above, but I had my own private entrance. At the main level was a wraparound porch with a great railing, occupied most early evenings by my beach friends hanging on it like a bunch of monkeys. Ocean City was very safe for us then; we could have dunes parties with bonfires, we could go to the nearby bars, lie about our ages, drink beer and dance, we could stay out late and go for fried chicken at Violet's after-hours place, and nobody worried about us. Muggings and other evils were unheard of. It was a wonderful way to spend one's summer, especially in the company of a tall blond boyfriend named Bernie, who was a terrific dancer. I did a lot of unaccompanied singing too, whenever anyone asked me, including once at a fashion show at the Henlopen Hotel in Rehoboth, and often while sitting on some friend's porch in the dark. People sat on their porches a lot in those days, before television took over our lives, and I was enough of a ham to relish the applause from other darkened porches up and down the street.

At sixteen, I obtained a summer job (thanks to Dad's connections) with an insurance company in the city. I typed into little forms all day – grateful for the one commercial course I had opted for – and rode the bus and streetcar two hours each way, each day, to reach their offices in the city. Although I had my driver's license by then, I was not permitted the exclusive use of the car I loved, which was the station wagon with wooden sides. The commute was a real drag, but I enjoyed the independence and especially the paycheck.

Meanwhile, continuing in our war efforts, my friend Susie (Anita Lou) Susemihl and I, who had been taking voice lessons, drove ourselves each Sunday to the USO downtown to sing for the servicemen there. At that point in my life, I didn't know whether I wanted to become an actress, an opera singer or go into musicals on the Broadway stage, but Susie knew. She went on to study at the Peabody Institute, while I chose a liberal arts education, because I really didn't know. Even today, my friend and Goucher roommate, Annelle, and I, will say that we don't know what we want to be when we grow up. I think the underlying force that propelled me was to live a normal life unencumbered by mental illness.

I was never a debutante, never "came out" as many young girls did in the city, at the Bachelors Cotillion. I was only an ordinary small-town girl, and the most we ever did as a debut to society was to have a sweet-sixteen party at the Glyndon Women's Club. I even missed out on that because of my mother's mental health.

Mine was altogether, however, a happy childhood, very likely much happier than that of my little brother, who bore the brunt of life with Mother after I had departed for college. This hardship didn't prevent him from graduating on time from Johns Hopkins University. Later, he attended law school, practiced in Towson for many years and wound up his career with many more years as a circuit court judge. His first marriage, like mine, ended in divorce but left him with two talented, handsome sons who have families of their own today. Chris's re-marriage to Judy has endured for many years, and today my sister-in-law and I are close friends.

Chapter 5

In my nineteenth year, when I was home for Christmas vacation, our grandfather died of a heart attack in his car, just outside our driveway. I remember standing beside my mother as we watched him depart, as the vehicle cane slowly to a stop. She gripped my hand and whispered "Oh, no!" and then shouted for my father. It was all over in seconds, and we did not know about his battle with angina until the nitroglycerine tablets were later discovered among his belongings. He was sixty-eight years old.

Also during my nineteenth year, while spending most of my summer at the Oregon Swim Club in Cockeysville, I had met John. He and I dated for two years and had become quite intent upon a future together, when I realized that I could not bring myself to convert to his Catholic religion – which in those days was pretty much a requirement for a girl if she wanted to marry a Catholic boy. I just couldn't do it, in addition to pledging any future offspring, as well, to the church. Unexpected reinforcement of my position came from Great-Uncle Norman Meese who, as a thirty-third degree Mason, informed me that he could not attend my wedding if I were to marry a Catholic. I loved and respected my uncle, which made my decision even more painful.

Chapter 6

I had spent my first two post- high school years at the women's college of Rutgers University, now known as Douglass. New York was within easy reach by train, and every now and then I met my dad in New York when he was there on business. Once, he took me to dinner at a night spot called the Rainbow Room, and we danced to the music of Tommy Dorsey. A music major at the beginning of college, I was excited to be so close to New York with all of its infinite possibilities; but somewhere along the way, my yearning for the normal life took over from my musical ambitions. I changed my major, first to psychology, then to English, and transferred to Goucher College in Baltimore as a junior,. This was largely to be nearer to home, where the family felt I could be useful during Mother's collapses. At that time, Goucher was just constructing its campus in Towson, so we transfers had to spend our first semester living in the city and commuting for classes to the county, an awkward arrangement which soon changed to allow us residence in the new Mary Fisher Hall on the county campus. My roommate, Annelle Kitchen from Alabama, had been selected for me, but she turned out to be a terrific roommate, and our friendship remains close even now.

Annelle invited me to spend our Spring break at her home in Montgomery, where I was beautifully entertained in true southern fashion and met some charming boys. One of them, a student at Auburn University, wrote a poem for me. I guess he found something interesting about the Yankee visitor.

One semester was spent living at home because Mother felt

that she needed me closer, although I can hardly recall any specifics about that need. I had to commute to classes, using her car, (which displeased her greatly), from home to the city each day. This arrangement changed, happily for me, when the next semester began, and I was allowed to return to the Goucher campus in Towson.

In 1948, when Dad became a delegate to the Democratic National Convention in Philadelphia, he invited me to come along and observe the process of nominating a presidential candidate. I sat aloft in the press box with Bradford Jacobs from the Baltimore Sun, fascinated by the excitement as Harry Truman distinguished himself by delivering an unexpectedly rousing speech after he became the nominee.

No longer a particularly dedicated student, I involved myself in musical and acting performances whenever an opportunity was presented. My favorite acting memory is playing the part of Eliza in *Pygmalion*, a show we did in collaboration with students from Johns Hopkins. I had another good role, the mother, in *Our Hearts Were Young and Gay*. There were others, and I sang in choirs and choruses and was perfectly content with average grades. My degree was in English. I had zero interest in graduate school, with my sights set on the real world. I fancied, like many young people, that I could do something really worthwhile and make a difference for mankind. I had spent a couple of summers and semester breaks modeling and in sales for Hutzler's department store. I was one of the models for Hutzler's first televised fashion show, wearing the requisite brown lipstick which would show up better on the screen. But I declined the store's offer of a career in retail leading to a position as buyer. It seemed a frivolous future at the time. Making a difference in the world would require quite a different approach to life, I decided.

Chapter 7

Following graduation, another good college buddy and I, along with a friend of hers who was new to me, embarked upon our first trip abroad. We sailed to Europe on a "student" (cheap) ship bound for the Grand Tour. Unfortunately, the other friend's parents had prevailed and we were stuck on what was then known as a Cook's Tour – the company who were believed to provide a safe and secure manner of travel for innocent young ladies at the time.

To my great good fortune, my very favorite and close cousin, Norman Meese, was studying at the University of Neuchatel in Switzerland, and had offered me refuge if the Cook's Tour became intolerable. It did, as we were leaving the French Riviera, and I simply jumped ship (so to speak) and fled to Neuchatel and Cousin Norman.

The last days of the Cook's Tour were not without drama, however. The three of us took a train from Nice to Monaco, intent upon some fun at the Monte Carlo casino, which we did enjoy, but we missed the last train back to Nice and had to spend the night on the grass under some trees in a small park just outside the casino. Meanwhile, we had met up with a Dartmouth student who borrowed twenty bucks from me, bucks which of course I never saw again. Waking at dawn in the park was a memorable event, to say the least. Soon after that adventure I said goodbye to my friends and headed for Switzerland.

The town of Neuchatel is situated on the shore of Lake Neuchatel, with beaches in several spots along its banks that are accessible by streetcar a short distance from the center of the municipality. At its center is the Hotel du Lac, a favorite gathering place for students of the university which was named for the town. Outdoor tables with umbrellas are plentiful, and it was at one of those tables that I found my cousin, along with several of his housemates, drinking tea with rum or a cold beer. Classes were over for the semester; it was time to party.

Norman had arranged a "pension" for me at a short streetcar ride's distance from the town center. He accompanied me so that I could be properly introduced to the home's owners, who were to be addressed as Monsieur and Madame. The latter, being a very proper Swiss-French lady, was deemed a suitable chaperone for the visiting American girl, whose parents might be quite upset at the turn of events which had brought her here. Madame very kindly showed me to a charming room, from whose windows I could enjoy the scents wafting from the nearby chocolate factory. Each morning she brought me a fresh croissant or brioche, along with a pot of hot chocolate. Then I would bathe, dress, gather up my swim gear and head off in search of my cousin and his boys.

How could poor Norman know that the wealthy Swede he had in mind for me would not be my type, and that I would instead fall head over heels for the American from New York with the moth-eaten woolen swimsuit? Twenty-eight years old, Freddy Klaus, whose childhood had been spent in both the States and Yugoslavia, had grown into a sophisticated, bi-lingual and irresistible charmer. From the first moment of our meeting I was lost. Freddy had the attributes of a pied piper. All of the temporary ex-pats in that circle in Switzerland, and later everywhere else, wanted to be with Freddy. Naturally, where he led us all was often into trouble but, at that age, nobody cared.

One night the gang went to an after-hours club to continue

our partying. As we ordered drinks, Freddy realized he had left his wallet behind in the restaurant where we'd dined. He left to retrieve it, only to discover that the club entrance was now closed and he would not be allowed to re-enter. Ever resourceful, he found a ladder tall enough to reach to an upper window in the building, climbed it and, after jumping down from the inside of that window, appeared once again at our table. I was very impressed, as his reason for such persistence was me. I believe that was the moment we became a couple. Freddy was not only resourceful, but mysterious as well, which naturally deepened my attraction to him. He told me he'd been in the Army Air Corps as a fighter pilot, which would of course explain his status as a beneficiary of the G.I. Bill, enabling him to study there in Switzerland. When I inquired about his "wings", he said he had given them to the young son of a girlfriend he'd spent some time with in Capri, and I believed him. Before we parted, he for New York for a family emergency, I for Paris, he had proposed and I had, tentatively, accepted. At the time, it didn't occur to me that he might be capable of enormous fabrication.

I was incredibly naïve. How I managed to survive alone in Paris for several weeks is today a mystery to me. Freddy stayed in the city for a few days before his departure for New York, but after he left I was truly alone. There were a few acquaintances from the short stay in Neuchatel – a couple of South Americans from Colombia, a couple of Americans, but no one close. So I bought a dog, a miniature French poodle named Zeno, who unfortunately developed distemper, and died shortly after I had acquired him. By November, I was ready to go home.

When my ship docked in New York, I had already overstayed my scheduled time in Europe, and my parents were eager to greet me. They were not so eager to meet this new young man who had entered my life but, as was his talent, he quickly had them under his spell. We had dinner together, the four of us, and I came home to Maryland glowing with the prospect of Freddy's visiting us very soon for a week-end. He did, of course, and that was soon followed by my visit to New York to meet his family. The first question by his eleven-year-old niece, Marilyn, was whether I had met Grandma and Grandpa. Imagine my shock at the question: Freddy had informed me while in Europe that they were both dead. You can also imagine the conversation later. I was too young and naive, and too much in love, to abandon the relationship then and there, and Fred had explanations for everything. For his parents' continuing existence, he had been ashamed of their immigrant status. I was also a bit stunned when little Marilyn advised me I would be going to Hell because I wore lipstick.

Freddy's strange background had also forbidden music, the theatre, art and certainly the use of alcohol. All of these strictures had been thrown off completely by the time I met him. My soul mate, I thought, who could enjoy the opera with me as well as all of my other cultural pursuits. And he did, easily convincing me that the days of prevarication were over. I learned to love his parents, with Mama trying to teach me how to make strudel, and Papa manufacturing his own schnapps. He wasn't constrained at all by his wife's religious beliefs. I once accompanied her to church, where I gained a whole new perspective on religious practices like "speaking in tongues" and falling to the floor in worshipful ecstacy.

Gradually, the partially true story came out. Mama had mistakenly believed that she was automatically included in her husband's American citizenship. When they returned to their farm in Yugoslavia, situated in a German section of the country, she had no defense when the Serbs overran their town and took her prisoner, and Papa had no resources to set her free. It took a lot of diplomatic hoopla on the part of American-born Fred and his brother, Louis, to get their mother out. I was told that she made most of the trip to Switzerland on foot to meet her son and fly back to the U.S. This, too, was never entirely clear. Sometimes it was said that Mama had escaped the camp on her own, which would explain walking across Europe, but details were always murky. In going through our later correspondence from Innsbruck, I've rediscovered that Freddy always anticipated a financial settlement from the Yugoslavian government for the suffering of his mother but, to my knowledge, it never appeared.

As for Freddy's wartime service, he attained the rank of corporal as a member of a medical squad, having been drafted to serve in World War II. He was legitimately entitled to the G.I. Bill benefits, but the glamorous fighter pilot didn't exist.

Chapter 8

Both parents, Dad especially, urged me to remain living at home until I could decide which way to attack adulthood, but I was determined to proceed independently and without their supervision. The first task, of course, was to obtain employment so that I could begin to support myself. Marrying Freddy would be my real future, I thought, but meanwhile it would be wise to try my wings. First, I visited a college friend who was living in New York City, spending several days checking out the want ads before I became depressed by the idea of living in a studio apartment with a view of a dirty brick wall from my friend's lone window. The whole idea of New York was, at the time, depressing when I thought of my lovely, spacious home in Maryland.

So I joined several friends from Goucher in renting an apartment in Baltimore, on Calvert Street, in an old but very large row house occupied by its elderly owners. They lived on the first floor and we had the second, which had been outfitted with a kitchen and consisted otherwise of a living room and three bedrooms, with one bathroom to be shared by all of us girls.

Finding a job, the first challenge, was not very easy. I interviewed at a printing company which produced mainly restaurant menus, and I would have been proofreading there for what seemed like hardly any money at all. I said no to that one, then applied to the Department of Education – never having aimed at teaching– and was hired to teach the fourth grade at Montebello School, a sort of experimental institution where the students were well-motivated and eager to learn. My sights, however, were set on a wedding, and by Spring I was out of the apartment, out of the teaching business, and married. In April, with Dad in public office, we had decided on a small family-only affair, and I had wanted to be wed by our former priest from All Saints Episcopal Church in Reisterstown. "Toby" Johnston had been transferred to another church in Frederick, Maryland, and that is where we were joined. At the time, it was a "dry" town, so we transported sparkling burgundy (my favorite instead of champagne) to the hotel for the reception. We had really scaled it down in order to avoid the publicity which Dad's position would have engendered in our own territory, but gifts arrived anyway, many from people looking to influence the Chairman of the Board of County Commissioners. I know this sounds cynical, but it's true, and it's why we tried to keep everything as simple as possible.

Freddy promised me a honeymoon sometime in the future. We spent our wedding night in the Dutch Village Motel on the way to New York, where one of his relatives had agreed to lend us an apartment in Queens, and where Fred had a job waiting for him with his brother's knitting factory. Although this apartment was also depressing, I took walks in the neighborhood and traveled to Manhattan by subway, and just enjoyed the idea of being part of the adult world.

My new husband was never cut out to work in a knitting, or any other kind of factory. When Dad announced his intention to run again for public office in the coming Fall election, we dropped everything in New York and returned to Towson to help, albeit as salaried employees! But the real plan, ultimately, was to find a way back to Europe as soon as possible, and with that in mind we moved to Washington when the election was over, to begin researching possible ways of achieving that goal. We took strange jobs: I tried door-to-door cosmetic sales and a switchboard at Travelers' Insurance Company; Fred sold advertising space for the "I am an American" day parade. I auditioned for a commercial with Willis Conover and got beaten out by Betty White (I had never even seen a television commercial at the time). Fred applied for and was accepted into a government project called the "Kreis Offizier" program. The idea was to send young American couples to German-speaking countries to promote socializing between the two societies. Freddy was completely bi-lingual and a natural for this kind of outreach. However, funding was never achieved, and in the end he decided to again take advantage of the G.I. Bill. He selected the University of Innsbruck, in Austria.

Chapter 9

I have often said that I would not trade the following two years for anything. Our stay in Innsbruck, beginning in the winter of 1950, when Austria was still suffering the many after-effects of World War II, began with culture shock and ended two years later in a mixed bag of emotions upon our departure. I carry in my memory a black and white picture of a building viewed from our arriving train, its side sheared off and bedsprings hanging precariously from the exposed rooms. Then, as we departed the train station, we looked up through crisp Alpine air at the snowy peaks of the north chain, the mountain range separating Austria from Germany. I would be awestruck again and again by those mountains, for we found an apartment from whose balcony we could see them every day. Never mind that the balcony had no railings. The newly-constructed house belonged to a young couple who were paying for it over time from the husband's salary as a baker in the nearby village.

The Dietrichs, Thilde and Richard, became our very good friends during our stay in their second-floor apartment. Our quarters consisted of a bedroom, a living/dining room, and bath shared with the host family. In the bathtub we washed our dishes and bathed when necessary. The Dietrichs, including their two-year-old toddler, Peter, also used the bath when necessary, although they had a small lavatory on the first floor for basic needs. We were lucky. Most of the friends we made at the university lived in rented rooms and had no choice but to frequent the public baths. We quickly became accustomed to the European way - once a week for serious bathing was quite enough. This new house also boasted central heating, and electricity was available for us to cook on a two-burner, using the pressure cooker I had insisted on bringing with us from the States. We missed a few other Stateside amenities, such as real toilet paper and Kleenex, both unavailable in post-war Europe.

So we became members of, and leaders of (thanks to Freddy the pied piper) the colony of foreign students making their way through the University of Innsbruck. There were several other Americans, one or two Brits and a couple of Swedes. Most of our group came from the U.S. One couple, Jackie and Dmitri Bhoutsas, resurface many years later in print, when Jackie and I both appeared in the 1974 edition of Who's Who of American Women. Another of our friends was Kurt Schuschnigg, named for his father who had been Chancellor of Austria from 1934-38, just before Nazi Germany annexed the country.

I must admit that cheap meals at the University's cafeteria quickly lost their appeal for me when I encountered a wheelbarrow full of calves' heads on its way to the campus. We had the advantage of the U.S. government's G.I. Bill supplement - $100 per month, which was sufficient for our rent, food and libations in the local restaurants. Needing no new clothing except for an occasional sweater or some underwear, we could use the surplus for travel, and that we did. Ski lift tickets, on student rates, ate up very little of the monthly allotment, and the fees at the university were so negligible as to matter little, and I enrolled at the university along with Fred. Austria covered us with its socialized medical program (mostly) and, until I encountered a female medical issue necessitating a stay in the hospital, we had virtually no medical expenses. We were young, invincible and of course convinced we would never have such problems.

For Freddy, the first order of business, after registering for classes, was to try out the local ski slopes. It being a sport I had never even dreamed of trying, the learning curve took more than a little while. Outfitted with a shiny new pair of wooden skis and leather boots, I proceeded nervously to the baby slope of the nearest mountain - which we could reach by streetcar, carrying the skis over our shoulders and depositing them by our sides once aboard the car. I then awaited instruction from my experienced husband. I was terrified to realize that getting to the baby slope involved riding in a chair lift, and getting on and off it with the new skis attached to my feet. However, that worked out and I made a few tentative slides, pointing toes together in a very basic snowplow. As I stood resting and working up the nerve to proceed farther downhill, a female speed demon swooped past me, over the tips of my skis, severing them completely from the parts on which I stood. She came to a stop at the bottom, looked back and realized what had happened. Freddy, meanwhile, had sped down after her and, in the course of their animated conversation, it was agreed that she would pay for the repairs. I couldn't believe they could actually repair these wooden sticks, but the next day the laminate was complete and I was back at it again. I never became an accomplished skier, but got just good enough to really enjoy it and not be terrified. Good enough, that is, to make a few stupid moves, one of which nearly cost me my life.

One sunny day, as we made our schussing way down a forested path, I tried a steep turn and missed, sliding instead off the trail and into a snowfield that overhung a treacherous cliff. I landed hip-deep in powder just short of where the cliff sliced the mountain. Freddy yelled to me to stay put, take off the skis and wait. He removed his skis, came gingerly to me, took my hand and my skis, and led me carefully back to the trail. Scary? Yes. Endearing? That too. My hero!

Habits formed; friendships melded; our life in the Tyrol became a beautiful patchwork of fun, study, travel and, for me, some homesickness. As I review my letters to my parents at home, I realize how much I missed what we had left behind. At the same time, however, I was relieved to be far from the turmoil caused by my mother's festering psychosis – until she decided to pay us a visit.

Before that fateful day, little brother Chris came to spend the summer with us. At fifteen, he was a long-limbed, gangly sprout, full of curiosity and ready for adventure. Too bad we had to spend part of that summer with Fred catching up on some courses in summer school. We lucked out in finding it possible to achieve the goal by his enrolling at the University of Vienna summer program at Gmunden, in upper Austria, where we located an apartment over a garage near the lake. Of course, it had no bathroom, only a courtyard fountain and a privy attached to the garage. We shared it with our Swedish friend Ake Orndahl, and every meal had to be in a restaurant, although we managed breakfast "at home." Our transportation that summer was by Ake's very large and accommodating motorcycle – the four of us onboard wherever we went.

Ake (pronounced Ohka) was also attending the summer school, so he and Freddy went off to school each morning, leaving Chris and me to find our own amusement. Most days we went sailing, renting small craft that we thought we could manage – little sloops that overturned easily and dumped us out into the lake. We were frequently rescued from the sudden storms appearing out of nowhere from over the mountaintops, and hauled back to the dock upside-down, but laughing all the way. It seemed as though our years aboard the Nancy Lee had prepared us for this adventure.

In my letters home later in the summer, I complained to Dad that my brother was bored with our lifestyle, wanting more action and entertainment and, I know, returned home somewhat disappointed in his visit to us. I think the lack of ready cash and the necessity for summer school played a part in this, but I for one was delighted to have him around for a while. He later remedied his gaps in European joie de vivre by returning on his own a few years afterward, as attested to by his own letters.

Chapter 10

We then awaited the visit from Mother, who arrived via the Queen Mary and expected one or both of us to meet her ship. Which I did by myself for reasons forgotten – probably having to do with lack of money. As I watched my mother descend from the ship, I was only happy to see her, little suspecting the daunting weeks ahead. After the short train trip from LeHavre to Paris, where I had booked a hotel for us for a couple of nights (so that she could see Paris a bit) we seemed happily compatible. Shopping, sightseeing, escorted around the city to locals' haunts by our friend Jess Hahn, who knew the best cheap restaurants. Jess even got us tickets to a Christian Dior fashion opening where I fell in love with the fragrance Miss Dior – which permeated the House of Dior at the time.

Two days into Mother's visit, however, I began to sense the alarms. On the overnight Arlberg Express back to Innsbruck, she slept not at all and woke me repeatedly asking the names of mountains or lakes or towns we passed through in the pitch black. I knew we were in trouble, but didn't realize how deeply until we got her settled, more or less, in the Maria Theresien Hotel in the center of Innsbruck. It was the best one we could find for her, since we had no guest accommodations at our tiny apartment in the village of Amras.

It wasn't long before even our medical student friends began to notice some strange behavior and suggested sleeping pills in her after-dinner coffee, which did nothing to induce a night of slumber. I was already exhausted from the first few days with her, and the two of us realized very soon that we could not leave her alone in the hotel, but had to move into her room in order to keep watch. She had begun to wander the town, looking for signals from her "boss," the CIA, in the form of green colors (on coats, buildings, anything), reds (similarly) and yellows (also) and at one point, having gained access to a home by claiming some bizarre signal, she began locking the inhabitants in their rooms, which resulted in a frantic call to the local police. We already had them on notice of the missing woman, so all was readily smoothed over, but the ordeal was far from finished.

Austria was then controlled by four powers: the U.S., Russia, France and Britain. As luck would have it, this was the Russians' turn to run the show from Vienna, which compounded the difficulty of reaching anyone by phone from where we were. It took several frantic cables before we were finally successful in reaching my father to arrange Mother's departure, by air, accompanied by a nurse trained in psychiatric care. Mother had to be persuaded that her doctor needed her at home for some mysterious mission, and we took her by train to Zurich, as there were no functioning airports in Austria at the time. Finally, the nightmare ended and we returned to normal.

Normal, for our cadre of foreign students, meant morning classes, long lunches at the Goldene Rose in the city's old section, the Altstadt, followed often by a trip to the slopes in winter or to the nearby lake in summer. Evenings were devoted to movies – John Wayne dubbed in German helped me learn the language – concerts or games of charades in the bar of a hotel that catered to American military personnel stationed near Innsbruck. We became close friends with the director of the USIS (United States Information Service), who offered me a job teaching English to local Austrians. It paid very little, but was nonetheless rewarding as I grew very fond of my adult students and felt challenged by their provocative questions (What happened at Little Rock and what does it mean? Can you explain the black/white population difficulties?) When the course was over, they presented me with a volume of photos of Innsbruck, delivered with many hugs and fond wishes.

We auditioned for the chorus at the opera house's production of Verdi's Aida, and both were accepted. I was still serious about my vocal career and had found a voice coach who worked with me on the Aida as well as Violetta in La Traviata and Mimi in La Boheme.

The next summer, the Austrian government invited us to star in a travel film which was designed to attract tourists. Called Mein Sommer in Ober Oestereich, (My Summer in Upper Austria), it took us from the Tyrol through Upper Austria and on to Vienna, me riding in the limo with the producer and his assistant, and the photographer, but poor Freddy following behind on a Puchroller – an Austrian motor scooter. In the film, we supposedly used the scooter for transportation throughout the trip. We were wined and dined most generously, all of our expenses paid including those incurred when I developed a tapeworm and had to spend three days hospitalized in Mondsee. Everyone had wondered why I had such a hearty appetite and remained slim and trim. Of course, the worm was getting most of my steaks. It finally emerged at twenty-three feet, as described by my doctor when he brought it in to show me, wrapped around his wrist.

It seems I had been foolish enough to eat beef tartare in North Africa when we'd been there earlier in the year. What a trip that was! Along with two other couples and a few more of the gang,

Lois Baldwin DeVoe

we traveled to Sicily, enjoyed a few sunny days in Taormina in a lovely hotel high above the sea, then embarked on a voyage by third- or fourth-class ship to Spanish Morrocco. The overnight accommodations lacked even rudimentary comforts; men and women were assigned to separate bunkrooms where all but the hardiest became seasick in their bunks, and the rest of us spent the rainy night sitting out the storm on deck. All were drenched and miserable by morning, and grateful for the sight of land. I remember being in Tetuan with Freddy, roaming the Casbah and being offered hits from a communal pipe as we sat in a circle of strangers. I remember declining, and Freddy accepting, and then he was so spaced out that I had great difficulty getting him out of there and back to our hotel. A young boy named Mustafa led us back, and became our guide for the entire stay. I don't recall eating the raw beef, only what it caused later.

Another memory surfaces here, of a second trip to Sicily and North Africa, a trip highlighted by a stop in Palermo, where we visited the catacombs and were duly horrified by the hundreds of dry, hanging mummies. No hashish on that occasion, but on the return we got a glimpse of Gibraltar, which rounded out my experience in the Mediterranean to some extent.

At the end of our film-making tour we were paid a very nice salary, which disappeared from Freddy's inside jacket pocket when he handed our baggage to me in the train compartment, as we were departing Vienna. Any plans we'd had for that nice little treasure had to be abandoned, and of course the thief was never apprehended.

I have the album of "still" shots that was given to us at the end of our film tour. It reminds me that some of our scenes were shot in a monastery occupied by an order of monks who were sworn to silence. Only their social liaison, Pater Willibrord, was allowed to converse with us, and that he did, showing us around the buildings and grounds and entertaining us with wine and cheese and great discussions on politics and religion. I was honored to be the first woman ever permitted to touch the silver chalice in the chapel, and there's a photo in the album to illustrate the fact. Pater Willibrord also took us to a remote camp in the woods, where he retrieved a months-old loaf of bread, still edible, for some strange reason having been preserved by the remarkable environment of the camp.

Somewhere along the way I was filmed in a bubble bath, part of a visit to a spa. Dr. Zenthofer, the producer, using his cane to try and push more bubbles away from my nude body, remains a vivid memory of that occasion. Had the old man not been accompanied by his assistant, who we discovered was also his mistress, I fear that he might have begun making passes at me in the limo, with Freddy safely toiling along behind us on the Puchroller. We heard the old rascal and his girlfriend in the bathtub together one night, which erased all doubt as to the Fraulein's position in the company.

A true highlight of the filming tour was attending the Salzburg Festival, particularly the famous play *Jedermann*, performed at night in an open amphitheatre. This was as exciting as seeing opera in Rome at the Baths of Caracalla had been for me on my first European trip. I can still hear the mournful cry "Jedermann" echoing from the walls around us, although I can no longer recall what it was about, other than the fate of every man – (Jedermann).

Losing our money would have upset us a great deal more had it occurred when we were back in the States. Our material needs were sufficiently provided for; we had no household or children to support, no cars, no need for new clothing as long as the old was not threadbare. Haircuts were very cheap, I didn't wear make-up then, only lipstick if I remembered; food and drinks were quite affordable, as were ski lift tickets, movies and local transportation. Health insurance was provided by the Austrian government, and for long distance travel we could frequently rely upon our thumbs. So a one-hundred-dollar monthly stipend from the G.I. Bill took very good care of us.

There was a U.S. Army base near the town, from which American soldiers on leave would emerge to seek some fun at the local bars and restaurants. One was a café within a park, containing a large bar that featured many gleaming bottles reflected in the mirror behind the bartenders. Our group liked to hang out there and, one evening, as we passed by a lonely-looking black soldier, one of the Swedes invited him to join us at our table. In my previous world, in segregated Maryland, such a thing would have been unthinkable. However, he came and sat at our table, and asked each of the girls in turn to dance. I said to Freddy, "Do I have to?" and his reply was that it would be rude to refuse. So I accepted the offer to dance with the black soldier, whereupon one of the white soldiers at the bar wanted to know who was the white whore the black guy was dancing with then…and Fred replied that that was his wife, and took a swing at the white guy. Things erupted very quickly after that: bottles smashed against the mirrored backdrop, glass shattered, scuffles and punches and shouting and cursing and, finally, whistles and the arrival of the Military Police. We students scurried out before they could stop us, and escaped to safety in the park outside. I never forgot, though, that the black soldier had pushed himself against me as we danced, and I was pushing him away just when the fight began.

Chapter 11

After almost two years, Freddy still hadn't completed his education and I was aware of a growing restlessness. Like treading water, I sometimes thought. We should be settling down, starting a family, paying attention to career goals, and generally behaving like adults. But the lure of European life remained strong in both, and we decided to try Vienna for a while, perhaps finding jobs with the U.S. government presence there. We were really fortunate when our friend, Hedy Brossard, arranged for us to sub-let an apartment normally occupied by an American boyfriend of hers, who had taken an assignment for our government in another country for an extended period of time. Joe would be happy to have his place lived in and looked after. We were happy to oblige, and so began our six months in the Austrian capital. The year, 1953, was four years after the filming in Vienna of the movie The Third Man, and the city looked much the same as it does in the film: dark, dreary, war weary and war-torn. The apartment, in the Ersten Bezirk, or First Circle, was well located, spacious, up one flight of stairs, and had an actual kitchen, full bath, drawing room with a piano, a large bedroom and, although not in service, a telephone. For heat, a woodstove had been left with an ample supply of logs, and every morning it was Freddy's job to fire up the stove to make the place warm enough for me to venture out of bed.

Public transportation was sketchy at best. We walked everywhere, often past the bombed-out opera house as well as other demolished cultural icons: statues, churches, parks. Vienna, at the time, seemed a sad shadow of its former self. Nevertheless, things still hummed in the U.S. headquarters, as evidenced by the summons we received from our American ambassador to wire the family at home immediately. Yes, we had failed to write upon arrival in Vienna, and Dad was really upset. So some of the money we had planned to spend at Christmas went to Western Union, and we decorated our tree with candles. Somehow, after viewing it at a local art gallery, we managed to scrape up enough to buy a painting we'd both fallen in love with – a crayon (art supplies being limited in post-war Vienna) rendering of a frightened alley cat. It reminded us of the devastated city itself, and I had the picture still, hanging in my loft where I did my deskwork, until we made the move back to Baltimore. But that's part of another story and my painting now resides in my son's home.

Concert tickets were cheap. We did a lot of concert-going. We looked for work. I was tentatively offered a position which would have required government clearance. We thought about it long and hard and, in the end, decided it was time, after all, to return to the States.

The journey home, as I wrote in a previous chapter, took us by a circuitous, heartbreaking route. It was so hard to sever ties with the continent we'd grown to love so much. It had been so effortless, as well, to experience other cultures - Spain, including Madrid, Barcelona and the islands of Majorca and Ibiza, French and Spanish Morocco, Sicily with its own uniqueness, Paris and other parts of France, London, Germany, Italy. Yet we felt that we had only scratched the surface of travel possibilities. Going home, facing up to adulthood, would signal the end of most of those possibilities.

I didn't realize it at the time, but it was also the beginning of the end for our marriage as well.

Chapter 12

Following the lingering travelogue of our last few weeks on the beloved continent, coming home to Towson brought us down to reality with a thud. A place to live, jobs, making new friends, all challenges to be addressed now without delay. As always, Dad came through with a job for each of us in his real estate business, and found a nice little house for us to rent in nearby Cockeysville. Freddy worked on "the draw" meaning he could get advance payment on commissions as yet unearned, and was released into the selling field where he excelled. I, on the other hand, became an unwilling office worker with unrealized yearnings to be out there in the selling field too. Years later, the tables turned somewhat and my urge to sell bore some fruit, in another era, almost another life.

Meanwhile, Dad decided to locate his real estate and insurance office in the lower level of a house on Joppa Road which he had purchased when he and Lucy married. Fred and I had by then escorted my mother to Mexico, at her insistence, so that she could obtain a divorce. Sad though it was, I've always admired my mother's decision to do this because, as she said, "I want him to have a chance at happiness, and I can't be a help to him in my mental condition." These are not her exact words, but the meaning was clear: she wanted to be out of his way so that he could marry again, someone whose sanity remained intact. And so he did. In his last years, suffering from what was assumed to be Alzheimer's disease, my father was cared for faithfully and lovingly by my stepmother, Lucy, and for that I am eternally grateful to her. She loved the man, unquestionably, and stood by him in his darkest hours politically and in his declining health. Nineteen years apart in age, they enjoyed a good life together, traveling to places neither had ever visited, working together in the political arena where Dad once again held the highest office in Baltimore County, and to their great joy, producing two sons, Michael and Peter, both close to the ages of my own children - who made their appearance in the next phase of my life.

Politics attracted us both, as we became members of the Young Democrats of Baltimore Count and I, somewhat surprised, was elected Vice-President of that organization. From there, I became a special assistant to the President of the Young Democrats of Maryland, and then National Committeewoman, a post that took me to Washington on occasion for conferences and meetings. I should add here that, while in Europe, we were both followers of the Gary Davis "One World" movement, which called for abolishing passports and allowing everyone to move freely about the globe. We were, I suppose one could say, almost flaming liberals. Now, back in the States, we found a home with the Young Democrats.

At some point during this period, between 1953 and 1956, we learned that I was definitely unable to become pregnant because both fallopian tubes were hopelessly blocked. Test after test showed no hope for a normal course of events for me. I won't say that this led to the unraveling of our marriage, but it certainly was a factor. We both wanted children; we had waited because we wanted to be settled first, and be able to provide for a family. But when it was not to be, we began to drift apart.

Still unwilling to give up our ties to Europe, we managed to return every winter to Austria to ski. One year, while in Kitzbuhel, we became good friends with a Belgian couple who were traveling with a writer friend. Sabine and I took a day off from the slopes to go shopping and to visit a fortune teller, a palm reader she had heard about. She emerged from the session very upset and wouldn't reveal why. She finally confided in me that someone close to them was headed for an automobile accident and that the outcome would not be good. We met them again the following year, when she then told me that their writer friend had been killed in a car crash during the previous year. The accuracy of the seer's prediction was borne out. I have mercifully forgotten her predictions for me, but I gained a new respect for the fortune-teller's art.

At home, we developed a close friendship with a couple who lived on Tyson Street, then the best-known artists' colony in Baltimore. Every house was painted a different color, and Jane and Alvin's had been remodeled so that their kitchen faced the street and their living room the walled garden at the back. Many martinis and steaks were consumed there by the four of us. Two childless couples in our late twenties, we did everything together from attending museum events to traveling the state on the Maryland House and Garden Tour. Jane and I each drove an MG TD sports car, tops down except in rain. We spent days at Oregon Ridge Lake, sharing our life stories, or sometimes continuing the remodeling of her house on Tyson. One day we got carried away by the possibility of a fireplace to be discovered behind a wall in their bedroom, using crowbars and raising buckets of dust as we tore away at the plaster. Sadly, there was no fireplace to be found, but when the husbands arrived from work there was plenty of shock and dismay at the mess we'd made. Our party group consisted of several other couples, some with offspring, some not, and nearly all of these couples eventually became uncoupled, including ourselves.

When we separated, not exactly amicably, I set out to make a new life for myself. I was devastated by the new knowledge of my own disability which, I thought, would discourage any possible future suitors who might have the desire to father a family. I took a job as a legal secretary, shared housing with my brother Chris, and waited out the year until my divorce became final. It was during that year that I discovered there was, in fact, one young man who had different ideas about fathering a family.

Chapter 13

I first met Billy Baldwin when we were teenagers and our fathers ambitious political figures in the Democratic party. His Dad, H. Streett Baldwin, the undisputed "Boss" of his organization, had taken an interest in the young Christian H. Kahl and was in fact grooming him to take over the local leadership as Streett moved on to a national position. In time, my Dad became that local leader when Streett was elected to Congress but was reluctant to give up his local power and the two became arch rivals. Billy and I never became friends during that period. In fact, during one recount of paper ballots after yet another bitterly-fought primary election, we found ourselves on opposite sides as "challengers" - a job entailing attempts to disqualify ballots because of some real or trumped-up flaw in the way an X had been penciled into the box next to a chosen candidate. Those ballots were then ruled upon by a three-mad board of election judges who had been appointed, not elected. One can imagine the ensuing power struggle to determine winners.

When we met again, years later during my separation from Freddy, our fathers had by then reconciled their differences and been elected to the same three-man board of county commissioners, with Streett replacing my father as chairman, since one of his followers had been elected instead of one of Chris Kahl's. Streett passed away while in office, at the age of 58, from a stroke. I've always felt that the loss of his two oldest sons during World War II was a contributing factor to his early death. The remaining two sons, Maurice and the baby of the family, Billy, were allowed to remain at home to run the farm. His sister, Mary Louise – "Wesi" - was three years older, and Maurice had been born two years or so before her, so Billy was truly the baby. Tail-end Willie, he had once called himself in a high school essay.

After the untimely death of Streett Baldwin, his man Michael J. Birmingham became chairman of the commissioner board, but soon the movement toward a different form of county government succeeded. With the voters' approval, the new government called for a County Executive as top leader, and seven members of a county council. Birmingham was "grandfathered" into the executive post for the remainder of his term. In 1958, my father ran against him and became the first elected County Executive of Baltimore County.

On one of our first dates, Bill took me flying in his Piper Tri-pacer, a single-engine four-seater. Even though his older brothers had both been killed in the Army Air Corps, he and Maurice were determined to learn to fly. Billy was a very competent pilot; I had no fear and enjoyed the experience very much. Of course, I had had no fear when my buddy, Danny Duncan, took me flying while we were still in high school. Danny was a beginning student pilot, which I didn't know at the time, as we swooped and buzzed our neighboring houses in Reisterstown. In hindsight, I should have been petrified but, at the time, it seemed just a fun way to spend a summer afternoon.

After the divorce, when I was working in Washington and living the single life in Georgetown, I had some interesting dates. : a Washington lawyer from New Orleans who loved to play tennis and often took me out to dinner; a Secret Service agent who liked to dance at a local military officers' club; Baltimore Sun reporter David Culhane, who later worked for Charles Kurault and appeared on his Sunday morning television show. David traveled with the press corps attached to Russian president Nikita Krushchev when he visited the United States and told me afterward that the man was "a muffin", apparently very congenial. I had good friends in Georgetown: my college roommate Annelle Murray and her husband Jim, another Goucher alumna, Ruth Hamilton, and one of our medical student buddies from Innsbruck, Gregg Rhodes, who was doing his residency in a D.C. hospital. I was also contacted by an old boyfriend from Rutgers, who had become a professor at Temple University and had some business in the District at the time. When we met again, it was gratifying to note that I had not made a mistake in breaking up with him years before.

During that time, Bill would often call me to meet him at a nearby airport to go flying. It was during this period that he proposed and I declined, saying that I didn't think we had enough in common to make a go of marriage. However, when I told him about my devastating fertility problem, his response was that we could always adopt. This I never forgot, and when we finally did marry a year and a half later, after a disastrous reconciliation with my first husband, we began almost immediately shaping pans to do just that.

My friend Lydia has often said that we got the cream of the crop because of our family connections. Maybe she was right. Our two adopted kids, Nancy and Streett, have grown up into the most amazing adults, loving, responsible, successful, good-looking and both the apples of my eye in every way. Billy didn't live long enough to see the finished product, but he would be very proud of them, as am I. We had both been convinced that, although heredity played a major role, the environment in which a child grew up was at least equally important. Our families embraced them with instant love. And we two, even through our troubled marriage, loved them fiercely. I still do.

We married in 1960, at Dad and Lucy's home in Four Winds (Towson) in a very simple ceremony presided over by my old high school friend the Rev. Fred Eckhardt, followed by a simple reception and a honeymoon trip to Virginia Beach by way of the Old Bay Line down the Chesapeake. We settled in an apartment near the Towson University campus, and I went to work for Judge John Grason Turnbull as his judicial secretary. I became good friends with one of Bill's associates in his law office, Jacke McCurdy, who remains my good friend today. It had been Jacke who accompanied me to Alabama for the final divorce from Freddy Klaus, and it was Jacke who served as my maid of honor at the wedding to Billy.

The Piper Tri-pacer had by then been replace by another Piper Tri-pacer, after a devastating snowstorm had demolished the roof of its hangar and crushed the little plane beyond repair. We decided I needed to learn to fly, just in case. So I took lessons and soloed, although not without a near disaster. As I rounded the pattern at our small airport, Rutherford, and turned to final approach, another, slower plane cut me off and I was forced to either crash into him or go around again and re-do everything. It was a bit scary being alone in the air and without radio contact, but the re-do was successful and my landing smooth. As onlookers came rushing toward me, I assumed there would be accolades and applause for my perfect landing; however, everyone rushed past, toward the upside-down Piper Super Cub at the end of the runway, containing the errant pilot and two ladies, all of whom had miraculously escaped injury. With such a happy ending, we headed for the nearest bar and my congratulatory drink.

Bill then traded in the Piper for a Cessna Skylane, a more

complicated aircraft with autopilot, which I could still handle in the air, but its complexity dampened my enthusiasm for obtaining my license and, besides, I was preparing to become a mother.

In the meantime, a couple of Bill's buddies also learned to fly. It must have been a big craze at the time, because my college roommate, Annelle Murray, did the same and I actually witnessed her solo flight at an airport in suburban Washington, D.C.

Chapter 14

At the urging of a couple we were friendly with, who lived in the country nearby, , we moved from the apartment to a two-bedroom stone cottage on Falls Road near Cockeysville. It was a tenant house, had needed updating in a number of ways, and the task was completed by the owners of the farm on which it sat. Charm "oozed from every pore" of this little house, with its two huge fireplaces, its stone interior walls and deep windowsills, its paneled dining room, its tiny attic reached by a tiny staircase, and even its tiny kitchen and single bathroom. We brought our first dog home to this house. Schnitzel, a standard year-old female dachshund, was there to welcome our first baby when we brought him home. Schnitzie had no fertility problem; she and Willie, who belonged to our country friends the Opfers, managed, with a little help from our vet, to become parents of six lovely puppies. One of those little charmers proved so irresistible that we couldn't let her go, but kept her as a companion to her mother. We named her Quieken, (pronounced Keeken) because she was so squeaky as a baby. As you see, I was still living in my head in a German-speaking country, plus these were obviously dogs of German origin.

From this house, Streett learned to swim in the landlords' pool, and I watched a mare give birth in the field behind our house while waiting for the vet I had been instructed to call in the event. It was to this house that my friend from Switzerland, Tony Crivelli, came with his wife Monique, to visit us and plan for a cross-country trip in our airplane. Tony being a pilot with SwissAir at the time made the idea quite feasible. All of this came before the arrival of our son and before the unbelievable and tragic deaths of our Swiss friends in an auto-train collision in their hometown of Neuchatel later that year.

We had never stopped flying and now, we kept the plane at a neighbor's airstrip. I believe we thought that flying, after what had happened to Tony and Monique, was actually safer than driving. Statistics still seem to bear out that belief.

It was about then that my father offered us a gift of an old farmhouse on property he was developing, called Green Hill Farm, along with enough land that we could have our own airstrip. Unthinkable, for Billy Baldwin, to move to Reisterstown when all his life he'd known only the Long Green Valley and Towson. I have always wondered why I didn't press harder for this; for me, it would have meant back home again. Maybe I felt that I had moved on too far to return.

Meanwhile, our little boy was growing and making us proud of his every move. Each day, Bill would call me from the office to ask what new trick the baby had performed, and was he talking yet, and was he walking yet? He was a curious child, who loved taking things apart – like cigarettes, watches – but had no desire to put them back together again.

It was a beautiful time in my life, taking care of and loving this perfect little creature who had chosen us to be his parents. But we were eagerly seeking another baby, and knew we would need a more spacious dwelling, with things like laundry facilities and kitchen appliances.

So we began the search for the right home, and it turned up soon enough, but not before a disheartening experience with attempted land purchases and house plans. First, we tried to buy a lovely rancher with several acres adjoining the Opfers' farm, but someone else came in with a higher offer. Next, we tried for a ten-acres parcel at the southern border of the farm where our rented cottage stood, and someone else got that one too. Then, we found a newly-subdivided five-acre lot facing south on Belfast Road. Dick Opfer, our building contractor friend, drew up a set of plans for the house - a traditional colonial with the possibility of a wing, eventually, on either side. Needing approval from the developers seemed simple enough; however, it seems they never really intended to develop this land. They wanted a county road through it to a higher site owned by a friend or relative of one partner and, once that was approved, they found one thing after another wrong wit our plans until Billy, thoroughly disgusted, gave up the fight. To my knowledge, that property remains undeveloped even today, some sixty-five or more years later.

    I started looking, with the aid of a seasoned real estate agent we knew. His steering me toward Towson turned out to be a wise move.

Chapter 15

The house we found on Campbell Lane, in Towson, was perfectly suited to a growing family. Nancy arrived in our lives two years later, a beautiful three-month-old eleven-pounder. We had named Streett after his paternal grandfather as well as Billy's older brother and a long line of "Streetts" in the family. Nancy's name came from my side, for my uncle's young wife who had died far too early, leaving her three-month-old daughter without a mother. She was Anne Dixon; Nancy, the diminutive of Anne followed by my own name, Lois, seemed the perfect way to go for our little one. I had adored Anne, who was beautiful and much-loved by her husband, and had been lost to us at the age of twenty-nine. Her death was a mystery to me for many years, until her grown daughter, Betty Anne, researched hospital records and discovered that she had died from an infection. Was it acquired at the hospital? No one knows for sure, but I believe in today's world she could have been saved.

So now we had a plane-full. When we took the children flying, Nancy would always fall asleep easily in the back seat. Streett liked sitting in front with his Dad, who encouraged him to take the controls. I must admit this set my nerves on edge and, unlike Nancy, I did not fall asleep, ever, in the air.

Eventually, the Cessna Skylane gave way to a cheaper craft, which Bill owned with a friend, and finally the flying ceased altogether as we became interested in motorcycles. Beginning with a Yamaha 250 trailbike, Bill and a group of male friends would meet to ride on Sunday mornings. My jealousy drove me to beg for a ride through the woods, which he allowed me after much cajoling. He plantied me on the rear of his bike on some tied-down pillows. He took me over some really rough terrain, hoping to discourage me, but it didn't work. I was hooked, and wanted a bike of my own so that I could go riding with some of my female friends. One Christmas, never to be forgotten, he surprised me with a Yamaha 125, kept hidden in a friend's barn until after he had presented me with the owner's manual, all wrapped up in a Christmas package. That year, we took the bikes to Daytona, to watch our friend Gary Nixon, who was Number One in the world at that time for motorcycle racing. Gary had already suffered an incredible number of broken body parts, but it never slowed him down as he joined the newly-formed Baltimore County Trailriders Association and participated in all of their motocross events. We used to joke that the groups consisted of a bunch of middle-aged men whose fathers would never let them ride motorcycles as kids. Now they were lawyers, doctors, insurance or real estate brokers, and many of their wives, myself included, became enthusiastic riders as well, as did our children. Nancy and I even acquired a couple of small trophies to prove the point. And, instead of playing bridge on, say, a Thursday morning, we would trailer our bikes to the local bike shop and take off up the railroad tracks to reach the Loch Raven woods and hit the fire trails there. We often stopped at Peerce's Plantation for a beer and a sandwich at lunchtime, where the ladies at the bridge tables in the dining room gave us curious, disapproving looks as we hung our helmets on coat-hooks at the bar.

As the kids developed the urge to ride, we got each of ours a little Yamaha 75. We kept them in a shed on our one-acre property, which was next door to the Towson YMCA and proved too tempting to someone who had a yen for a small trailbike as well as a big one. Two were stolen, one to be recovered after I put out flyers at all of the local schools, and the other – Bill's 250, - replaced by an insurance claim. Not to be fooled again, my wily husband then installed tamper-resistant chains in the shed, and we were not robbed again, at least not from there.

After his sprained ankle and a dislocated shoulder, both sustained during motocross events, Bill decided the family fun on bikes was over, and the motorcycles were sold, not without howls of futile protest. I might have kept mine, but would have had to ride it on the roads to get anywhere, as the trailer vanished also. However, the next toy was a condo in Ocean City, pleasing everyone but too short-lived to become a part of our regular lives. That, too, was sold as we moved into the next phase – boats.

So far I had learned to ski, to fly, to drive a motorcycle, and now I was to learn all over again how to manage a floating condo. Our first cruiser was wooden, like the old Nancy Lee, but it had two engines as well as a more modern interior. At 32 feet, it was reasonably sea-worthy and slept the four of us comfortably. Billy decided to name it the "Beanbag" in some sort of combination naming thing, claiming that because his nickname, "Beans", was derived from his family's farm product, and a woman is sometimes referred to as a "bag" it was a perfect name. Soon enough, we traded the first Beanbag in for a fiberglass version with a flying bridge and even more modern interior. Most weeks I spent doing the boat laundry and preparing food for the week-ends, as we were aboard constantly during the summers. We joined the Baltimore Yacht Club, where the kids and I became active in all the island organization had to offer – the Junior Armada, the Mates, the opening week-end show. We had purchased a sailing dinghy which also sported a small motor, thus enabling us to anchor out and still connect to shore. Frequently, we rafted up with friends or relatives who had sailboats or houseboats, creating a strange-looking conglomerate but also cementing bonds that, for our children at least, have lasted a lifetime.

Brother Chris was one of those sailboat types. Once, he invited us out for a Sunday afternoon sail; Bill couldn't go, but Chris's kids and ours did and, although it was Fall and his family supplies had mostly been removed and taken home, it was a lovely day for a sail. However, no sooner were we out of the cove than a heavy fog descended and we couldn't find our way anywhere. Trying to head home with the use of foghorns, and with other boats in the same predicament, we finally gave up, anchored and waited for the fog to lift. It didn't. There we were for the night, with few blankets and no food except for a large can of peaches and one of spinach. There was also, however, a large bottle of Vodka to save the sanity of the adults. In the morning, when the fog had finally lifted, my brother's head ascended from the hatch and gave out a huge howl – we were within perhaps fifty feet of his very own slip!

The boating life diminished for us as a family when our teenagers discovered other pursuits and declined to join us on week-ends. We'd had a good run with it. Then, as a grown man, Streett came back to boats where he is firmly ensconced today – a very confident and accomplished skipper of his own 47-foot craft.

Chapter 16

While Streett was still a baby, my good friend Jean Opfer decided that I had nothing to do (except take care of my child), so she asked me to do some research for her on the feasibility of starting a thing called a "senior center" in Baltimore City. As president of the Junior League at the time, she and her members were trying to convince the city powers of the idea's worth, and were meeting with resistance. I wrote a report for her, which the League used as a tool of persuasion, and it eventually succeeded. With helpful funding from the private sector, the city's first senior center became a reality called the Waxter Center. My interest in the subject had been sparked.

Meanwhile, with my father at the head of government in Baltimore County, the notion of starting a senior center in the county began to take root. Our Health Department director went to Washington to attend a conference on problems of the aging and returned excited about the prospect. Dad couldn't involve me at the time (nepotism being frowned upon) but he did appoint one of his admirers, a very bright lady named Margaret Shock, as Chair of a newly-formed commission to study the matter. Margaret, the wife of a renowned gerontologist, became my mentor in the volunteer field and, as time went on and Dad was out of office, I replaced her as chair of the Baltimore County Senior Centers Board and, later, the Commission on Aging. Even after Margaret's retirement from the field, we continued to meet often for lunch and I could always rely on her for advice.

I was sent twice to Washington as a delegate to White House

Conferences on Aging, and I had the great satisfaction of seeing an entire network of senior centers blossom around the county. When the Erickson company wanted to build the Charlestown Retirement Community in Catonsville, the very first of its kind in the area, our Commission on Aging was requested to meet with the developer and make a recommendation for its approval by the county government. I remember that Margaret was a bit skeptical, commenting that she though they were out to make money. But the project went on, succeeded, and gave rise to a number of other similar projects that today are home to a great many seniors.

Later, when I was fifty-one and wanted to go back to work in a serious way, I was able to parlay that volunteer experience into being named Executive Director of the Baltimore County Commission on Arts and Sciences – for me, a dream job. For the first time in years, I received a regular paycheck, I had an office and a small staff, and I was involved in the cultural life of our area. Hired by then County Executive Don Hutchinson, I represented him on the Boards of many of the major cultural institutions of the city. We provided financial support to the Baltimore Symphony, the Baltimore Opera, the Baltimore Zoo, the Maryland Science Center, the Maryland Historical Society, the Walters Art Gallery, the Baltimore Museum of Art, the National Aquarium, and many others. The most stressful aspect of the job was defending my budget before the County Council, whose members sometimes had difficulty understanding why county dollars should be spent on supporting city organizations. The answer was simple, at least to me and the members of my commission who made the dollar recommendations. Our county surrounds the city; our residents are the major audiences for those attractions, because our county has precious few similar ones of its own. Part of my job was to continually monitor and evaluate the worth of these institutions and see how our money was spent. Each budget year, they all must file applications to be reviewed by the Commission and approved by the Executive before being assigned a cash figure in the annual budget. My staff and I did the prepping and the liaison; commission members reviewed applications and made recommendations, and after Executive review I went before the Council, sometimes to be humiliated, sometimes praised, but always with nerves on edge.

As a result of my position with the county, I was appointed to the Maryland State Arts Council, serving as a board member for several years. This pleasing, although minor, notoriety stands in stark contrast to the time when I was accused of censoring a student art show we had permitted to be displayed in the County Office Building - the censorship accusation stemming from removal of two works, one depicting a dead infant and the other a nude self-portrait. County officials had me explain, in radio, television and newspaper interviews, that the office building was not an art gallery but a public locale where citizen meetings took place, and that these two works might prove objectionable to some. Frankly, I disagreed, but could not afford to stand my ground on the issue. There were even embarrassing cartoons. Eventually the storm subsided, and life went on.

Another pleasing but demanding aspect of my job was to run the summer concert series at Oregon Ridge, the county-owned park in Hunt Valley where a pavilion had been erected to protect the stage where performances took place. These included the Baltimore Symphony, Baltimore Actors' Theatre, barbershop quartets, country bands and, at season's end, a festival we dubbed Sunday in the Park. Daughter Nancy became the chief, each summer, of my clean-up crew. Later, there was an attempt to build a larger facility, to protect the audience against rain, for we were often forced by weather predictions to cancel shows. The project won a referendum, but when it was determined that the neighborhood would not tolerate a connection to nearby public water and sewer facilities (due to fear of housing developments springing up in the valley) the approved funding went to the digging of wells and the installation of portable restrooms. Having worked so hard to create a true summer venue for our symphony orchestra, we were deeply disappointed.

It was after one of those summer concerts that Nancy and I returned home to find a message from my brother that our mother had passed away that evening. She had survived a stroke some two years before, had gone into a coma and been kept alive by machines and feeding tubes, then miraculously awakened from the coma as a normal person with normal brain function, and no more psychosis. She had then been transferred from the mental institution to a nursing home. There, she developed internal bleeding, probably a result of having been fed for so long by tube into her stomach. Chris and I had just visited her at the hospital where she'd been taken for treatment, and been advised that she was stable, that we could go home and get a good night's sleep. She obviously took a turn for the worse during the night. I have always deeply regretted that I was not there for her when she died, especially since she had emerged from the long bout of mental illness and been, once again, my mother.

They say that to write truthfully, one need only open a vein. It is true, and there is much pain in writing about things like the death of a parent. Our mother had spent a major part of her life in a a locked psychiatric ward, which was painful enough. Searingly painful, also, to write about the death of a marriage, but as it is a true part of the story here, I tell you now that Bill and I separated, twice, before his final illness brought me back into his life to care for him. We remained on good terms throughout the separations, continuing to share holidays and family vacations, but we lived separate lives. I eventually bought a little townhouse in Cockeysville after renting apartments for a while. Bill always blamed the feminist movement for our troubles. I blamed his drinking.

The kids went off to college. Streett got married, only to suffer a personal tragedy of his own when his new wife decided she wanted to end it. . Bill got lung cancer and lost two-thirds of one lung. He stopped smoking at last. I got breast cancer, in 1987, and have survived it. But Bill's cancer had metastasized to his brain, and in 1989 it killed him.

The nineteen-eighties were not good to me in many ways. I lost my mother, then my dad died of complications from Alzheimer's disease in 1985, and my husband passed away in the Fall of 1989, at the age of sixty-two.

Chapter 17

Democratic politics had been a part of the fabric of my entire life. Being married to a Baldwin only enhanced that, as Bill progressed from Towson lawyer to part-time magistrate, then to member of the Baltimore County Board of Appeals, and after that to the Maryland Public Service Commission – a body which regulates the utility companies – and finally to District Court judge. Earlier, he ran for the House of Delegates on the Democratic ticket, winning the primary but losing in the general election to a Republican. We had an exciting spring and summer during that campaign, and were naturally very disappointed at the outcome. When offered the judgeship, he finally found his niche and remained contented in the role for the rest of his life. Lots of "perks" came our way during the years, from one or another of his positions. We attended Lyndon Johnson's Inaugural Ball in the nation's capital; we traveled to Atlantic City before the casinos arrived, to Hawaii, New Orleans, San Diego, Mexico, Las Vegas and other destinations along the way. We were entertained lavishly by the utility companies wherever the Public Service Commission's conferences took place. We met Ted Kennedy and his then-wife, Joan, at a private party for an acquaintance who was running for Congress. Billy's father's story appeared in a new book "Marylanders Who Served the Nation" for his two terms in the House of Representatives.

The Baldwin family I had married into had suffered enormous tragedy during World War II: Billy's two oldest brothers both died while serving in the Air Corps. The remaining two sons, Maurice and Billy, were permitted, perhaps required, to stay home and manage the family farm. Their father continued his political career, returning from Washington to serve on the Board of County Commissioners with my father, his erstwhile arch-rival, only to suffer a stroke while in that office, and pass away at the age of fifty-eight.

His widow was the family matriarch when I joined the clan, and she welcomed me whole-heartedly, as she did our children when they arrived. I have the most loving and tender memories of Mary Baldwin, who was known fondly by the family as "Goo-goo". She had been left with very little money. She had needed to sell the family home, and sought employment to support herself, which she did for many years. She bought a small home in a community near Towson called Anneslie, where she entertained the entire family at Christmas. Her banquet table, with its many leaves, she brought with her from "The Wedge", the large country home she had shared with her late husband and their children – Streett, Wallace, Maurice, Mary Louise and Billy. The table overwhelmed her dining and living rooms, but it seated all of us for Christmas dinners except, of course, the little ones who had a special table of their own until they reached an age when they were allowed to join the adults at the big banquet table. Everyone had a pile of gifts to open; the bar offered not only whiskey sours and the usual cocktails, but also Goo-goo's special eggnog, the recipe for which is passed down to succeeding generations. Among the gifts we always looked forward to were her dozen jars of soup mix, containing the vegetables she'd procured at their peak during the season. She always said she would put everything in there except peas, which she did not care for at all. To make the delicious soup, all we needed to do was prepare the beef base. Imagine! Twelve quart jars of this wonderful soup mixture for each family – and that wasn't all. During the year, Mary Baldwin spent a lot of time knitting and crocheting special gifts like sweaters, capes, socks, even little crocheted containers for your chignon if you had long enough hair for it, which at the time I did. She was intelligent and well-educated, having graduated from what was then the State Teachers' College (now Towson University). She often said that her parents had thought it more important for her and her sister, Edith, to be properly educated than for her brothers, who would have the farm to support them. The girls needed a vocation, and so they both became teachers until they married.

I believe that when I separated from her son, proximity to my mother-in-law was probably the thing I missed the most.

Chapter 18

I must blame, or perhaps credit, Annelle for the next phase in my life. Through the purchase of a Volvo in Easton, Maryland, she and her husband, Jim Murray, had come into contact with our old buddy, Gregg Rhodes. As a medical student at the University of Innsbruck, Gregg had been one of our foreign student cadre during my stay there with Freddy Klaus, and had tried to assist us in our attempts to curtail my mother's wild careening into her manic condition during her visit with us there in Austria. Then, years later, a practicing physician in that Eastern Shore town, Gregg was recently divorced and was informed by the Murrays that I was recently separated. A few telephone calls later we met again, and thus began several bumpy years of on-again, off-again romance. We enjoyed some great trips together –Hong Kong and Thailand, St. Thomas, St. Maarten, Costa Rica, Europe two or three times. Things never went smoothly with Gregg; he could never be content with any woman close to his own age, which became apparent to my slow self only after several years. Meanwhile, however, I developed breast cancer and underwent a lumpectomy, and to his credit, Gregg remained in my life through that ordeal, and so did Bill. After the surgery and the radiation, my life returned to a fairly normal routine with work and travel and the long-distance relationship with Gregg, who was still in Easton and preparing to retire.

It was during this turbulent period that Billy had surgery for lung cancer but was able to return to work afterward. Two-thirds of one lung had been removed; he stopped smoking on the day of the surgery, but as it turned out the cancer metastasized to his brain and within three years he died. The last year I spent reunited with him and caring for him. Had he survived, I think we would very likely have reconciled, but it was not to be. On October 30, 1989, at the age of 62, Billy Baldwin was gone.

I continued to work at my job with the Arts Commission until the newly-elected Republican County Executive eliminated my position. So in January of 1992 I found myself unemployed at the very same time that daughter Nancy found herself also without a job. She was, of course, young and smart and easily re-hired by another tech company. I chose to become a wardrobe consultant for Doncaster, a company that does trunk showings in the homes of its sales force. Having bought and worn these clothes for several years, I found it a fun line of work; however, all my profits went into the purchase of more garments when not into travel. This was my decade for going places, with or without my friend Gregg. When he and I finally called it quits as he became enamored of a woman thirty years his junior, I kept on going places. Nancy, Lydia, Linda, Sandy, Jackie, son Streett, all joined me at various times on various trips: a hiking tour of Ireland, Alaska mainland and small ship through the inside passage, a cruise of the Mediterranean, a couple of visits to Mexico, Southern Europe, skiing in Utah, Barbados, Nassau, a poker cruise in the Caribbean, even Florida. I'd met up with another old friend who became my travel buddy as well – Bobby Knatz from Reisterstown. Life was good again, I was independent and blessed with good friends and a loving family. The Baldwin clan embraced every new man I brought to them, and so we continued the long-established traditions at Thanksgiving, Christmas and Easter and watched the next young generation grow up, go to college, get married and start families of their own.

My kids and I grew ever closer. Although off to a somewhat slow start, Streett got himself a CPA degree and began a serious career which has led him to partnership in a major Baltimore accounting firm, and home ownership in the up-scale Federal Hill section of our gritty old city. Nancy continued her education through her Master's in a program called Publications Design and Related Journalism, and today holds a leadership position with a technology company doing contractual work for the U.S. Government. She lives deep in the country with her companion of thirty years, Richard Deurer, two cats and several chickens. Both are in committed, although unmarried, relationships: Streett with Sidney Minor, Nancy with Dick . Both elected not to have children, although Sidney's daughter, Chelsea, kind of makes up for that in Streett's world. The travel bug has bitten them both very seriously. Nancy especially has out-done me in visiting exotic parts of the world.

And as for me? The next chapter in my long life began in August of 1999.

Chapter 19

The story of how Bob and I met and put our lives together has been told many times, to anyone who will listen, because to us it is amazing and miraculous that we found each other at this late stage, he at almost seventy and I at seventy-one. At this writing, we are approaching our fourteenth anniversary. Both of us had been widowed for ten years before we met. Both of our spouses had passed away in October of the same year, and we'd both been floundering around essentially alone for a decade.

Bob's oldest daughter, Kathy, had been telling me for some time that she wanted me to meet her dad, who was living in Atlanta at the time. I'd said that would be nice, and nothing happened. I continued to play golf at the Hunt Valley Club which I'd joined after retiring; Kathy was in my group, so we'd sometimes talk about how nice it would be if I could actually meet her dad. But whenever he visited her in her Baltimore County home, I would be somewhere else – Alaska, Europe, the Caribbean, and whenever I was around, at home, he was somewhere else – Russia, Africa; we were always in the wrong place at the wrong time.

Then two things happened. Bob became ill in Atlanta and Kathy insisted he com to live with her family. And she gave a party for one of our golf group who was moving away. I remember asking a friend from the group if she thought I should bring a date to the party, and being advised that Kathy's dad would be there. Obviously, no date came with me.

We spied each other across a crowded patio (I kid you not) and that was it. We sat for a long while talking about travel; he offered me a "real" drink – Scotch, instead of the wine and beer being served at the party. I said we should mingle because people were beginning to stare at us as we sat engrossed; he thought this was a brush-off. I came back asking for the Scotch, we talked some more and finally, when I was leaving, he showed me to my car and mentioned, casually, that he would like to take me to dinner. I said that would be nice. Then, I waited for the phone call for several days. When he finally did call to invite me out, he had been asking Kathy if it was too soon to call!

Six months later, we were married. Instantly, I became stepmother to seven handsome, bright adults and, at the same time, grandma to their seventeen offspring. As my children claimed, that let them "off the hook."

Chapter 20

We did everything backward: first, we honeymooned for two weeks in St. Martin. Then my kids had a reception for us at the Hunt Valley Club. After that, we were married at the Sherwood Episcopal Church in Cockeysville, where my former priest from Trinity in Towson, Kingsley Smith, was subbing for a time. Kingsley insisted that we attend Sunday services for a few weeks before he'd agree to do the job. I guess he thought we would take the whole thing more seriously if we had a few weeks' immersion in Scripture.

Starting off in this new life called for a new home, we decided, so after searching a bit we settled on Ruxton Crossing. Near Towson and conveniently located for everything we needed, and larger than my little townhouse in Cockeysville, the new place suited us very well for two years. We'd go to Ocean City and stay at my condo there on 64th Street, playing golf at various courses in the area, and gradually came to the conclusion that it might be nice to live on a golf course. It might also be a good idea for our new life as a couple if we struck out in a new direction together, making new friends together instead of relying solely on my old ones. This notion turned into a plan and, after our first two years as a married couple, we bought a "golf villa" at the River Run community just six miles from the Ocean City beach. For the first time in my life, I was able to choose everything for a new house: paint and carpet, appliances, upgrades and additions, and together we watched our new home grow into a finished product. My dream home had always had a second floor balcony overlooking a great room, so I naturally fell in love with the floor plan in which that was included.

With three bathrooms and two master suites, plus two additional bedrooms, we each had a private den to retreat to. A second-floor deck, a first-floor screened porch and a patio all gave us a constant view of the ninth fairway so that when not actually playing we could be watching other golfers.

Those were very happy years for us both, in this house on the golf course, and we hated to leave it – but leave it we must, while we were sill healthy enough to live independently in a retirement community, which would only admit us if we were independent. So we sold our home, and the memories of our life there come flooding back as I write this.

As the property lay along the St. Martin River (no relation to our favorite Caribbean island, but how appropriate a name!), and there was a marina for residents. I immediately started dreaming of a boat. The dream eventually became a reality when I bought brother Chris's old deckboat, named it the Lobo, and docked it within walking distance of our house. There were some disadvantages to the arrangement: our marina had no gas dock, although it did provide water and electricity, but for gas we needed to travel down the river and into the dock at the Ocean Pines Yacht Club – a forty-minute trip. And, although we boasted a "head" on board, there was no place at our marina to pump it out. I don't think we ever used that facility, but some good times were enjoyed on board. And for me, just "messing about in boats" was calming and pleasurable. Even to go down by myself to pump out the bilge and run the hose over the Lobo was a chore I looked forward to with pleasure.

However, it was only a year or so later that I developed the eye problem which plagues me still: macular degeneration. I first noticed something wrong as we returned from a vacation in Hilton

Head, with me at the wheel. I began seeing a double line instead of the single one painted on the right side of the road, and then some cobwebby features appeared in my vision. The diagnosis made by our local ophthalmologist was confirmed by a retinal specialist and he began treatment which has been going on for thirteen years in one form or another.

Unable now to distinguish a red buoy from a green at a distance, I confess it was a kind of relief when the Lobo refused to start up one day and had to be towed away for repairs. The season was over by the time she was ready to come back, and I put her on the market. She never sold, but was given away for charity and went to a good home in New England. I met the new owner as he came to retrieve his new boat, and was happy to observe that he seemed suitable.

Meanwhile, in our nearly fourteen years together, Bob and I had traveled some, although not nearly as much as we had originally anticipated when we first met. Canada, the Caribbean, Ohio, Michigan, Florida, Hilton Head, Sea Island, New York City and State, and Williamsburg, VA. That's about it, as we had grown older and more frail, and perhaps more contented to stay at home when traveling began to be more of a hassle than it was worth.

The River Run community is a unique one in its ability to give the residents a sense of belonging. Everyone comes from somewhere else, many not even from the state of Maryland, so we bonded very differently from people who grow up together in the same community. Whenever anyone falls ill or has an accident or surgery, the abundance of kind acts is incredible, from cooking meals to running errands, visiting, finding equipment, providing transportation or filling any other need. When I broke an ankle several years ago, my neighbors showed up with walkers, canes and crutches, a raised seat for the commode, even a portable wheelchair. Our wonderful next-door neighbors transported me in that wheelchair to the doctor's office as well as in and out of our house.

Yes, we hated to leave there, but that is not the end of the story. It is, however, the end of that chapter in my life.

We had lived at Mercy Ridge Retirement Community for over two years when my sweet husband passed away. A long-time smoker, he too developed lung cancer and left us only three weeks after the initial diagnosis revealed that probability as well as other problems which he had chosen to ignore. Letting nature take its course, I think he had faith that it was time, and he was very much at peace.

One week later, my beloved brother, Chris, succumbed to the results of several years battling ataxia, suffering a stroke that ended his life within a few days. He left behind his wife, Judy, with whom I have a close relationship, and his two sons, Chris and Andrew and their families.

But it has taken me three years to return to the completion of this book. This seems like the right place and time to end it, and if any of my readers feel that perhaps some juicy details are missing, I hope you aren't too disappointed. After all, I can't give away all of my secrets.

• *Photographs* •

Lois and Bob DeVoe

Hon. Christian H. Kahl, Baltimore County Executive

Lois and her mother

Lois and her little brother, Chris

Lois's parents

Nancy and Streett Baldwin

Lois's mother, Marion Kahl

Lois at 18

Captain Edgar Wells Meese (grandfather)

Bob and Lois DeVoe

*Hon. Christian M. Kahl judicial portrait
unveiling with wife Judy, sons Drew and Chris, and sister Lois*

Kahl Family Christmas Gathering 2019

Stepmother Lucy with Lois

Bill, Lois, Streett, and Nancy Baldwin

Brothers Pete and Mike

Brother Chris and nephews Drew and Chris

Baldwin Holiday Gathering - 2014

Lois's cat, Lucy

www.ingramcontent.com/pod-product-compliance
Lightning Source LLC
LaVergne TN
LVHW010308070426
835510LV00025B/3411